IPSWICH TO DISS

Including the Eye Branch

Richard Adderson and Graham Kenworthy

MP Middleton Press

*Front cover: Britannia 4-6-2 no. 70012 **John of Gaunt** climbs the bank towards Haughley station with the "Broadsman" express from Liverpool Street to Cromer in the summer of 1957. (I.C.Allen/Transport Treasury)*

*Back cover upper: No. 86237 **Sir Charles Halle** stands in the sunshine at the south end of Ipswich station with a Norwich to London train on 26th October 1991. (J.R.Sides)*

Back cover lower: No. 66558 has arrived at Barham aggregates terminal on 19th September 2007, with a train which had originated at Dowlow in the Peak District. (B.Steele)

Readers of this book may be interested in the following society:
Great Eastern Railway Society,
Peter Walker, Membership Secretary,
24 Bacons Drive,
Cuffley, Herts.
EN6 4DU

Published October 2015

ISBN 978 1 908174 81 9

© Middleton Press, 2015

Design Deborah Esher

Published by
    Middleton Press
    Easebourne Lane
    Midhurst
    West Sussex
    GU29 9AZ
Tel: 01730 813169
Fax: 01730 812601
Email: info@middletonpress.co.uk
www.middletonpress.co.uk

Printed in the United Kingdom by Henry Ling Limited, at the Dorset Press, Dorchester, DT1 1HD

CONTENTS

INDEX

ACKNOWLEDGEMENTS

In addition to those individuals acknowledged in the photographic credits, we are most grateful to Andy Fulcher, Mike Rayner, Dave Taylor and Andy Wright,

I. Railways of the area in 1954. Other maps in this volume are to a scale of 25 ins to 1 mile, unless otherwise stated, with north at the top. (Railway Magazine)

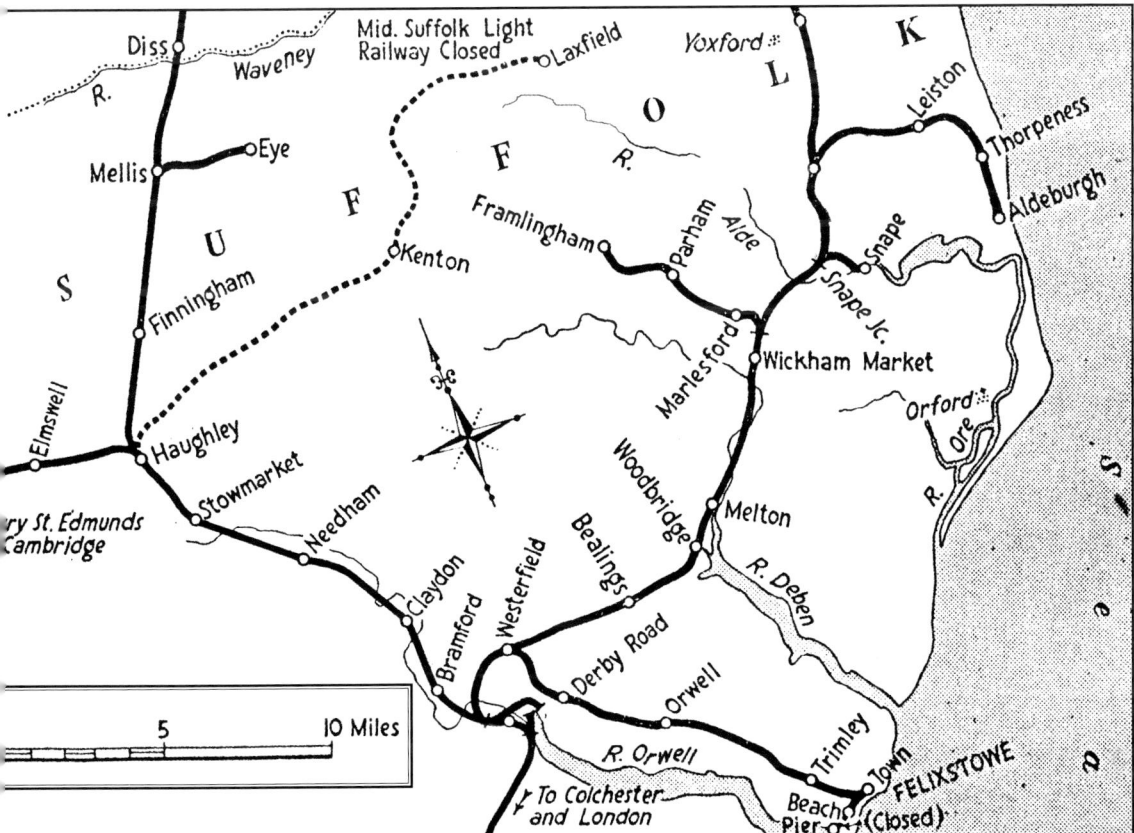

GEOGRAPHICAL SETTING

Ipswich to Diss

For the first 13 miles the route follows the valley of the River Gipping on gradually rising gradients. From a point just north of Stowmarket there comes a sharp rise for about four miles to reach the plateau formed by the underlying Crag; in crossing this higher ground, the line is straight for eight miles. A similar descent beyond Mellis takes the line down to the valley of the eastward flowing River Waveney just to the south of Diss station. This river marks the Suffolk/Norfolk county boundary.

Mellis to Eye

The River Dove, a short tributary of the River Waveney, flows through the eastern fringes of Eye. Consequently, the two mile long branch was largely on a falling gradient from the higher ground at the junction.

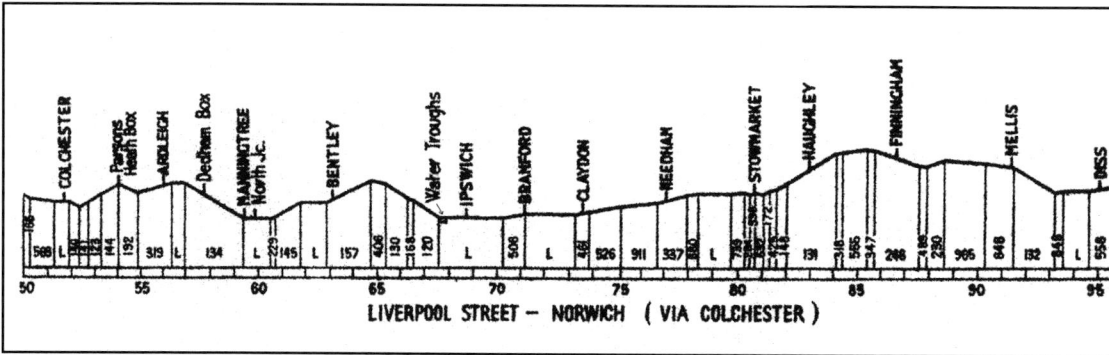

LIVERPOOL STREET — NORWICH (VIA COLCHESTER)

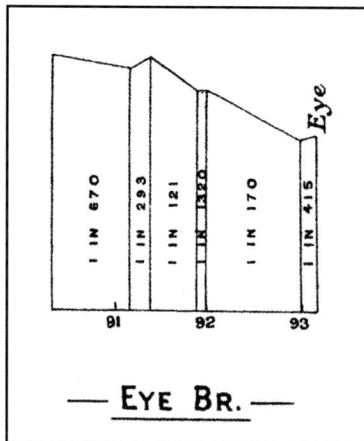

— EYE BR. —

HISTORICAL BACKGROUND

Ipswich to Diss

After a series of false starts on railway extensions from north-east Essex to south-east Suffolk, Ipswich was finally reached from Colchester in June 1846.

In the meantime an Ipswich & Bury Railway Act had been passed in 1845 for the onward development northwards, although the opening of this section was delayed, owing to difficulties with tunnel construction to the north of the first Ipswich station. Things were obviously moving rather more quickly early in 1846, as a further Ipswich & Bury Railway Act was passed in that year for construction of the final part of what became the main line from the junction at Haughley to Norwich.

The line via Haughley to Bury St. Edmunds opened on 24th December 1846, with that from Haughley to Diss and Norwich in two stages during 1849; to Burston on 2nd July and onwards to Norwich Victoria on 12th December. Trains to and from stations north of Ipswich continued to use the original terminal station until 1st July 1860 when the new through station was opened to the north of the tunnel.

Both developments north from Ipswich were under the management of the Eastern Union Railway, one of the five companies which were amalgamated to form the Great Eastern Railway in 1862.

On grouping, the Great Eastern Railway passed into the ownership of the London & North Eastern Railway on 1st January 1923, and the line became part of the Eastern Region of British Railways upon nationalisation on 1st January 1948.

After electrification north from Ipswich to Norwich, the full service from Liverpool Street to Norfolk's capital was introduced on 11th May 1987, although the section had been covered by the first electrically powered train just over a month earlier, on 6th April.

Following the changes which followed privatisation in the mid-1990s, services were provided by a succession of companies, using the brandings shown, as follows :-

5th January 1997	Anglia Railways
1st April 2004	one (National Express)
27th February 2008	National Express East Anglia (one rebranded)
5th February 2012	Greater Anglia (Abellio)
January 2014	Rebranded "Abellio Greater Anglia

Mellis to Eye

This short branch only three miles long was authorised by the Mellis & Eye Railway Act in 1865 in order to connect the market town of Eye with the increasingly important main line. It opened on 2nd April 1867. Although the branch was worked from the outset by the Great Eastern Railway, the Mellis & Eye Company was not actually absorbed by GER until 1898.

Following the 1923 grouping the LNER attempted to reduce the costs of passenger traffic by introducing conductor-guard working and opening a halt adjacent to the main road bridge in Yaxley. The attempt failed and passenger services were withdrawn on 2nd February 1931. Following nationalisation in 1948, freight traffic survived until 13th July 1964.

PASSENGER SERVICES

Ipswich to Diss

In 1848 the Ipswich & Bury Railway ran five trains from Ipswich to Bury providing services for stations from Bramford to Stowmarket inclusive. When the line from Haughley to Norwich was opened in December 1849, a further three daily trains were provided, taking just over five hours to connect Norfolk's county town with London.

By August 1863 there were seven trains from Ipswich to Diss, all of which called at Stowmarket, with varied calling patterns at the other intermediate stations. There was but one through service from Ipswich to Bury calling as required at all stations to Haughley.

This situation was much the same into the early 1880s. However, in later years, with services from Ipswich serving two routes diverging at Haughley, the stations south of the latter location were better placed to enjoy more attention than those to the north.

In 1920 there were eighteen trains from Ipswich serving Stowmarket, the main centre of population; of these, ten called at all of the intermediate stations and also at Haughley. Half of the eighteen went on to serve Diss, but with only six stopping at Finningham and Mellis.

Little changed through the 1920s and 1930s but, in the post-World War II years, a period of expansion of travel opportunities began. By 1950, Stowmarket enjoyed the provision of 25 trains from Ipswich, 13 of which went on to call at Diss, en route to Norwich. However, there were still only eleven services, including those heading to Bury, calling at the minor stations of Bramford, Claydon and Needham, with Finningham and Mellis still restricted to six.

This upward trend continued and in the Summer of 1964, by which time both Bramford and Claydon had closed, Stowmarket was served by no less than 32 trains from Ipswich, 15 of which went on to call at Diss en route to Norwich, with 17 heading for a range of destinations via Bury St. Edmunds. Needham and Haughley saw 13 of the 32 while Finningham and Mellis were restricted to about half of the Diss services.

Following the closure of the remaining minor stations in late 1966 and early 1967, the number of trains calling at Stowmarket and Diss showed a reduction to 10 each on the main line to Norwich, with Stowmarket hosting a further seven services heading onto the Bury line.

Electrification in 1987 introduced a timetable in which 18 main line services at broadly hourly intervals from Ipswich to Norwich called at both Stowmarket and Diss. Stowmarket received an additional 17 trains from Ipswich, destined for Bury and beyond; of these nine called at Needham Market, which had been reopened and renamed in 1971.

The 2015 timetable listed no less than 37 main line trains leaving Ipswich for Diss; of these, 28 called at Stowmarket, the other nine making connection at Ipswich with convenient Bury line services stopping at Stowmarket. The nine were included in the total of 26 Bury-bound services calling there, 19 of which also called at Needham.

Mellis to Eye

During the relatively short life of passenger services on the branch, almost all were timed to connect at Mellis with the fairly small number of main line services which stopped there. As noted above, this rarely amounted to more than six in each direction. In 1882, there were six branch line services with eight in 1920. A peak was reached in 1913 when there were ten.

1. Ipswich to Mellis

IPSWICH

II. This map, at a scale of 6 ins to 1 mile, dates from 1928 and shows the station opened by the Ipswich & Bury Railway when the route was extended from the first station to the south of the tunnel which is featured in our earlier volume Shenfield to Ipswich.

1.   Following a number of temporary operating arrangements, a permanent station was brought into use to the north of the tunnel in 1860. At first there was just the single platform seen here, but an island platform was added on the west side of the line in 1883.
(M&GN Circle, Marriott Collection)

2.   One day in the early 1920s, the spacious forecourt in front of the station is all but deserted. A number of cars, probably taxis, are parked in the middle distance, while a far more stylish vehicle stands in solitary splendour close to the main canopy. On the extreme right, an Ipswich Corporation tram does its best to elude the photographer, thus dating the picture before September 1923, when trolleybuses took over the services to the railway station. Ninety years later, a similar perspective can be obtained from a multi-storey car park, showing that the range of buildings is little changed, although the forecourt is considerably busier with road vehicles. (G.Austin collection)

3.   We are looking south towards the station during the Great Eastern era, with the railings of the bridge over Ancaster Road in the foreground. All the platforms are occupied, and in the midst of the bustle a horse is shunting a van on the middle road. Although partially obscured by steam from a tank locomotive, the large roof over the bay platform is a prominent feature. (R.J.Adderson collection)

4.   Work on replacing the canopy leaves part of the up platform open to the elements during the 1950s, giving us an uncluttered view of the main building as it approached its centenary. A tiny WH Smith bookstall is set in the wall, while the entrance to the platforms is behind the group of people immediately to the left of it. Contrasting with the grimy brickwork, the replacement awning, together with modern electric lighting, is taking shape to the right of the picture. (B.D.J.Walsh/GERS)

5.   "Britannia" class 4-6-2 no. 70011 *Hotspur* sets out for Norwich with the "Broadsman" express on 8th October 1952. From the start of the Winter timetable a few weeks earlier, this train, the 3.30 pm from Liverpool Street to Cromer and Sheringham, had been accelerated to cover the 115 miles from London to Norwich in an unprecedented two hours, including a three minute stop at Ipswich. (R.K.Blencowe collection)

6. The photographer has ventured beyond the shelter of the canopy to record the view looking southwards on a very wet 15th November 1959. (NRS Archive)

172   7 | 8 | 9 | 10   172
BRITISH RAILWAYS (E)   (Series 48)
5730   IPSWICH (A)   5730
PLATFORM TICKET 1d.
Available ONE HOUR or DAY of ISSUE only
NOT VALID IN TRAINS   NOT TRANSFERABLE
To be given up when leaving Platform
FOR CONDITIONS SEE BACK
1 | 2 | 3 | 4 | 5 | 6

(U.O.)   (U.O.)
British Transport Commission (E)
PARKING TICKET FOR MOTOR CAR
OR THREE-WHEELED VEHICLE AT
12 2010   IPSWICH   12 2010
Registration No.....................
Fee 1/0
Available on Day of Issue only.
FOR CONDITIONS SEE OVER

7.   Now we are looking northwards from the extremity of the island platform during the early 1960s, as one of the new BTH type 1 diesel locomotives runs through the station on the centre line. (NRS Archive)

8.   No. 47568 arrives with a Norwich to Liverpool Street train on 1st August 1985, passing no. 86243 *The Boys Brigade*, which is waiting to take the train on to London. The line south of Ipswich had been electrified since 13th May that year, and for the next two years it was the normal procedure for Norwich trains to change locomotives here. (R.J.Adderson)

9. Although the station has undergone many changes over the years, there has been no full-scale rebuilding. One such development was the provision of a second footbridge in 2012. A train for Norwich passes under the new structure on 19th March 2015, while the earlier footbridge still spans the tracks. (R.J.Adderson)

G. E. R.

Ipswich

IPSWICH LOWER YARD AND DOCKS

Map II also shows the branch which extended eastwards from a point adjacent to the passenger station to serve the Lower Yard and Docks. The first agreement for a siding facility was made in 1846 with William May, for access via what was referred to on an early document as the "Marsh Tramway" (later to serve what became the Lower Yard) to his premises adjacent to St. Peter's Dock immediately to the east of Stoke Bridge. The Lower Yard did not see any significant development until the mid-1860s, after which additions continued to be made until around 1920. The expansion of the Dock Tramway around the Wet Dock to serve a variety of businesses was a gradual process throughout the second half of the 19th century, but the full circuit was not completed until 1904.

10. No. D2281 attacks the sharply curved climb up to the goods yard from Ranelagh Road level crossing on 24th August 1968, with Ranelagh Road signal box next to the last vehicle. It is hauling a train of brake vans which has formed an enthusiasts' special over the docks lines. (I.C.Allen/Transport Treasury)

Other views of Ipswich can be found in -
Shenfield to Ipswich, Ipswich to Saxmundham,
Ipswich Tramways **and** *Ipswich Trolleybuses.* **(Middleton Press)**

11. Motorists on Ranelagh Road can only sit and watch as no. 03059 runs over the level crossing with a train from the docks on 27th March 1985. The lower storey of the signal box, complete with nameboard, remains in use. (R.J.Adderson)

12. Sometime around 1959, we are looking westwards from the bridge carrying Princes Street over the railway. Some wagons are being propelled towards the cattle pens, while Moy's coal yard occupies the area to the right of the picture. In addition, a long siding ran from the yard to serve the power station at nearby Constantine Road from 1903 until September 1954. (NRS Archive)

13. The tracks are becoming somewhat overgrown as no. 08661 approaches the bridge under Princes Street on its way to the docks on 30th August 1985. (S.McNae)

Extract from working instruction dated 11th December 1983.

BRITISH RAILWAYS
EASTERN REGION

INSTRUCTIONS FOR THE WORKING BETWEEN UPPER AND LOWER YARD AND FOR RANELAGH ROAD LEVEL CROSSING, IPSWICH

Bell, gong and telephone communication is provided between the Upper Yard Pointsman, the gate cabin, and Lower Yard Shunter.

The gates must be maintained and secured open to road traffic except when trains or vehicles require to pass along the railway.

14. We return to the viewpoint used in picture 3, but the photographer has now turned through some 90 degrees to record the docks branch on the far bank of the Orwell. Princes Street bridge is to the left of the photograph, with a number of cattle wagons partially obscured by the Lower Yard signal box. Further to the right, a GER tank engine goes about its business, while the three wagons next to it are a cosmopolitan collection, being lettered with the initials of their respective owners, the Midland, London and South Western and London and North Western Railways.
(G.Austin collection)

15. This view eastwards from Princes Street bridge shows the extent of the busy Lower Yard with the lines stretching away towards the docks complex. It is around 1959, and a Hunslet shunter is standing with a train of cattle wagons, while the large buildings in the distance mark the entrance to the docks. (NRS Archive)

16. As rail traffic declined, the redundant tracks were lifted piecemeal and the area was redeveloped. Retail units are encroaching on to the former railway land as no. 66141 stands in the remaining part of the yard with a train of limestone on 9th September 2000. This traffic ceased shortly afterwards, and by 2015 most traces of the Lower Yard had disappeared. (R.J.Adderson)

17. With the buildings along Commercial Road in the background, the enginemen on class J70 no. 68219 take it easy as their engine stands at the east end of the Lower Yard. Tram locos such as this were a familiar sight on the Ipswich dock lines from GER days until they were replaced by small diesel shunters in the 1950s, not long after this picture was taken. (W.J. Naunton)

18. A small shed, complete with coaling stage and water column, was provided for the tram locomotives at the east end of the Lower Yard. Class J70 0-6-0 no. 68222 was photographed outside the shed on 10th April 1954, its external condition matched only by the decrepitude of the building itself. By this time the diesels had arrived, and no. 68222, already the last of its type at Ipswich, would be withdrawn some nine months later. (R.K.Blencowe collection)

19. A gleaming diesel shunter, no. 11100, runs onto St Peters Wharf and enters the docks area during the early 1950s. It has just crossed Bridge Street, where, in previous years, the railway line had crossed the track of the Ipswich tramways system on the level. To the right of the picture, a siding, accessed by a wagon turntable on the line in the foreground, penetrates the gloomy interior of the former Oil Cake Mill. (R.E.Vincent/Transport Treasury)

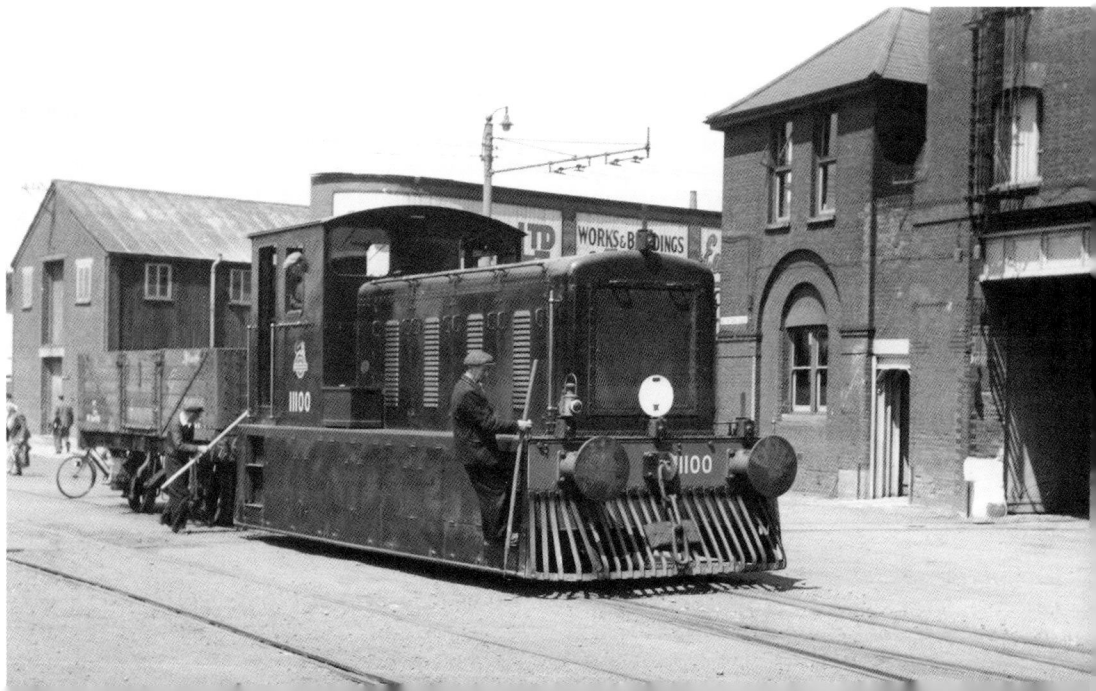

20. Here is no. 68219 again, this time emerging on to St Peter's Wharf from the colonnaded section of Albion Wharf underneath Cranfield's buildings on 20th June 1953. It is on the line which followed the north and east sides of the Wet Dock, while the tracks diverging to the right of the picture follow the east bank of the New Cut before rejoining the Wet Dock route at the approach to Cliff Quay. (RCTS Photo Archive, ref. FA10293)

Extract from Sectional Appendix January 1969.

IPSWICH DOCK BRANCH—PILOT QUAY

IPSWICH DOCK BRANCH—WORKING OVER PILOT QUAY VIA QUAYSIDE SIDING, EASTERN COUNTIES FARMERS, LTD. ELEVATOR AND TRANSPORTERS ON PILOT QUAY. Before passing the Eastern Counties Farmers, Ltd. Elevator and Transporters on the Pilot Quay, all locomotives and vehicles must stop and, before proceeding, the person in charge must assure himself that no one is standing between the stanchions supporting the Elevator and Transporters and the railway track.

21.   The waters of the Wet Dock are to the left of the picture, as no. 03059 runs along Orwell Quay (formerly Ransomes Wharf) on 18th February 1985. It is hauling a freightliner train heading for the Cliff Quay terminal. (S.McNae)

22.   On the other line, class J70 0-6-0 no. 68220 makes its way southwards along New Cut East on 6th August 1952. The Lock Tavern, which took its name from the original entrance to the Wet Dock, ceased to trade in 1955, while the Sailmaker's shop to the right of the loco adds to the maritime atmosphere. (R.E.Vincent/Transport Treasury)

23. Some fifteen years earlier, and a hundred yards or so further south, we find another J70 trundling along a deserted New Cut East with a train of tank wagons. The engine is lacking the protective skirts originally provided to hide the wheels and motion, and as other pictures confirm, this was the usual practice with the Ipswich tram locos in their later years.
(Suffolk Record Office, Ipswich, K681/1/262/507)

24. Closely pursued by a lorry, no. 08669 approaches the swing bridge over the Wet Dock entrance before reaching the junction with the more northerly line on an October day in 1985. Rail traffic in the dock area did not survive the 1990s, and in 2015 there were few tangible reminders of the network of running lines and sidings which once served the port and its industries. (S.McNae)

25. Two 0-6-0 tram locomotives, nos. 136 and 135, stand on the swing bridge in Great Eastern Railway days. The engines date from 1903, while the bridge is a year younger. A plate on the bridge shows it to be a product of Ransomes & Rapier Ltd, the well-known Ipswich engineering firm. The construction of the bridge completed the circuit of tracks around the Wet Dock. (R.J.Adderson collection)

Excerpt from LNER 1947 General Appendix.

DOCK BRANCH. DOCK COMMISSION SWING BRIDGE. General Conditions to be observed by all traffic.

(a) Speed restriction of 4 m.p.h.
(b) No train or engine may stop on the Bridge.
(c) No double heading of any train.
(d) Two empty wagons must always be placed between J. 66 or J. 67 engines and train, irrespective of load.
(e) One empty wagon must always be placed between tram engine and train, irrespective of load.

26. No. 08775 stands on Cliff Quay while working a brake van special for enthusiasts on 20th January 1990. The industrial environment is clearly seen. (D.C.Pearce)

B.R. 25559/1

BRITISH RAILWAYS

NOT TRANSFERABLE

FORM OF PERMIT

The Bearer Mr...R. ADDERSON............ ~~and ONE PERSON travelling in attendance~~ is/are authorised ~~on the payment of the appropriate fare(s)~~ to travel in the van with the Guard or in another vehicle not usually provided for the accommodation of passengers. CONDUCTED TOUR OF IPSWICH DOCK AREA

† { ~~By any British Railways Train~~
{ between IPSWICH MPD Station and return to IPSWICH MPD Station

subject to prior notice being given of each intended journey to the Station Master at the starting point ★ ~~(and to accommodation being available in non-passenger carrying vehicle by the selected service for the conveyance of the invalid vehicle)~~.

Valid ~~from~~ for 2¼ Aug. 19 68 to............... 19......

Signature of authorised Officer ....FOR DIVISIONAL MANAGER.

DIVISIONAL MANAGER .....H.L. Harrison

.....Station .....Region

GROSVENOR HOUSE Date 21. 8. 1968

★Delete if not required.   NORWICH   † Delete words not applicable.

27. No. 08661 waits as containers are loaded onto railway wagons at the Cliff Quay container terminal on 1st August 1985. At this time the terminal was in its second year of operation, but rail traffic would cease within seven years. (R.J.Adderson)

28. Our last view of the docks lines again features no. D2281 and the brake van special train in August 1968. This was the furthest point it reached, towards the south end of Cliff Quay, and the crew of the coaster moored alongside were somewhat amused to have their Saturday disturbed by the antics of a trainload of railway enthusiasts. (R.J.Adderson)

NORTH OF IPSWICH

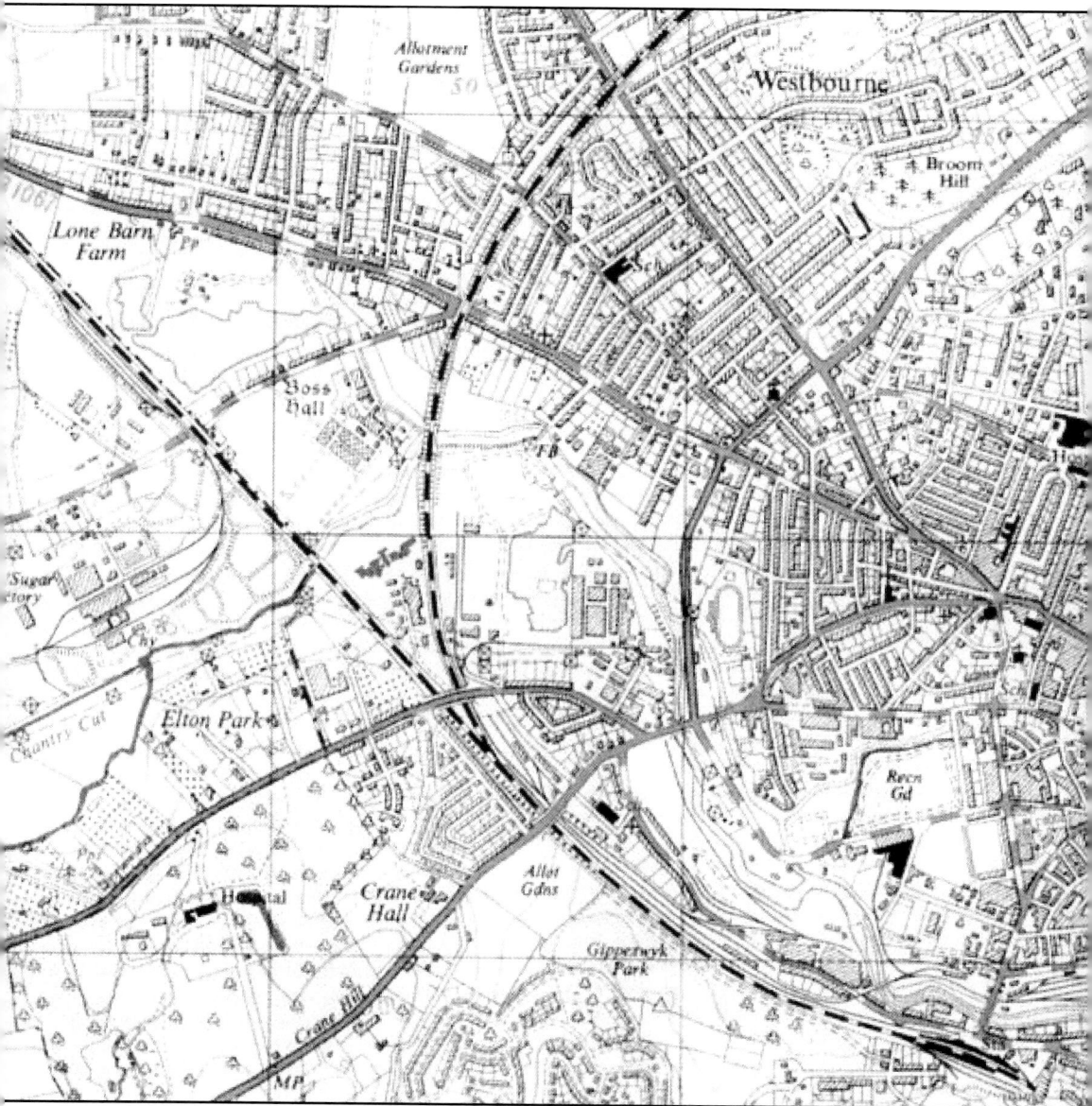

III. This 1950s map, at a scale of approx. 4 ins. to 1 mile, shows the site of the various yards that were northeast of the main line between the passenger station and East Suffolk Junction (featured in our earlier volume *Ipswich to Saxmundham*). Further to the northwest it also includes the 1920s sugar beet factory and the location of the 2014 "Bacon Factory Curve", which was provided for freight movements from Felixstowe towards the Midlands and the North without the complication of the change of direction in the freight sidings at Ipswich.

29. Class B12 4-6-0 no. 61569 nears Ipswich with a stopping train from Bury St Edmunds on 27th November 1954. It is passing under the impressive signal gantry, which had spanned six tracks on the approach to the station since 1912. Boasting no fewer than 20 signal arms, it survived until July 1957. Part of the transit shed can be seen to the right, beyond the tracks in Upper Yard. (P.J.Kelley)

30. Here is the transit shed five years or so later, around 1960. A Great Eastern signal still controls the exit from the docks line, and a vintage coach body serves some unspecified role in front of the shed, while two diesel locomotives are an early sign of the modernisation to come. (NRS Archive)

31. From 1913, a short goods branch spanned Ranelagh Road on this bridge, before descending steeply almost to the bank of the river. Ambitious plans to extend this line over the Orwell to connect with Lower Yard, thereby avoiding the level crossing on the busy Ranelagh Road, came to nothing. A trailing connection at the bottom of the incline led to a wide expanse of railway owned land which was never developed to any extent, although a few sidings served ramshackle timber warehouses until the 1960s. The tracks were lifted and the bridge demolished around 1967, just a few years after the date of this picture. (NRS Archive)

32. As traditional wagon load traffic declined, the Upper Yard assumed a new role in conjunction with the developing container traffic generated by the Port of Felixstowe. No. 47581 *Great Eastern* stands in the yard with a freightliner train on 15th June 1988, while no. 47572 *Ely Cathedral* waits on the main line with a similar train. The yard underwent considerable modernisation during 2014 to enable it to deal with demands of 21st century freightliner traffic. (R.J.Adderson)

33. No. 37216 and a class 08 shunter stand amongst the collection of buildings forming the engineers depot on 19th November 1992. This site had originated as a facility for dealing with the extra goods and cattle traffic generated by the 1934 Royal Agricultural Show, held nearby. After World War II it became the engineers yard, continuing in this role until 2014, when the area was redeveloped, remaining in railway use as offices. (R.J.Adderson)

Extracts from the LNER Magazine August 1934

Apart from the assembling and dispersal of the exhibits, the show brings with it a problem as to the visitors, many of whom come from long distances to visit the show. Extensive cheap-fare facilities were provided, and this, of course, carries with it the responsibility for having suitable train-service facilities available. Ordinary trains were strengthened, and in some cases duplicated, special expresses run from and to London, and no less than 31 excursion trains were provided, covering a very wide area. During the five days of the show, nearly 32,000 passengers arrived at Ipswich station,

When the train arrives at the show station, the job is not finished. A mile still separates the exhibits from the show ground, and here steps in the Cartage Department, with its modern equipment, a considerable amount of which has been assembled from various parts of the line. What the Cartage Department have to contend with can best perhaps be gauged from the maximum strength at work at one particular time. The heaviest day for the implement arrivals was on June 30, when there were 10 tractors, 6 mechanical horses, 30 trailers and 3 two-ton motors in operation. The livestock problem, a rush job throughout, is greatest during the dispersal of the animals after the show and, during the period of maximum pressure, there were 12 mechanical horses, 22 tractors, 12 Scammel floats, 18 tractor floats, and 6 two-ton motors in use.

34. The context of the Bacon Factory curve is best appreciated from above. Forming the third side of a triangle, the avoiding line curves sharply round from the new Boss Hall Junction, next to the river bridge on the East Suffolk line at top left of our picture. After recrossing the river, the newly-laid track runs parallel to the Norwich line for some distance before joining it at Europa Junction, another fresh name on the railway map. (M.Page)

GREAT EASTERN RAILWAY
ONE BICYCLE. Accompanied by passenger
At Company's limited risk rate.
[D.O] IPSWICH to
ANY STATION ON THE G. E. RY.
NOT EXCEEDING 25 MILES.
ZONE **25** Rate 6d.
Available for a single journey & on the day of issue
only & must be given up on completion of journey
[For conditions see back]

5448 5448

L. N. E. R.   L. N. E. R.
For conditions   For conditions
see back   see back
Available for three days   Available for three days
including day of issue.   including day of issue.
Ipswich D.O   Ipswich D.O
IPSWICH (D.O.) to
BRAMFORD
BRAMFORD   BRAMFORD
3rd. 6d.Z   3rd. 6d.Z

9783 9783

35.　The first revenue-earning train used the curve on 24th March 2014. Nine days later, we see no. 66732 hauling the 11.30 Felixstowe to Doncaster freightliner along the new line with what is still very much a construction site in the foreground. The tracks of the East Suffolk line are to the right of the picture, and it is interesting to compare this photograph with pictures 13 and 14 in our *Ipswich to Saxmundham* volume. (J.Day)

36.　This picture was taken at the convergence of the lines at Europa Junction, and gives an idea of the scale of the engineering works. We are looking southwards on 15th April 2014, and the route is set for the photographer's train to head round to Boss Hall Junction. (J.Day)

37. We now go back in time to 10th July 1929 and to a point just to the south of the future site of Europa Junction. The photographer has scaled a signal post to record signs of railway expansion in the vicinity of what was then Sproughton Lane level crossing. He is looking towards Bramford, and to the west of the main line a single track from the recently-built sugar beet factory crosses the road before dividing into a number of sidings, while a new and freshly ballasted goods loop diverges from the main line just north of the crossing. (J.Richardson collection)

From LNER working timetable October 1941,
hours of signal box opening on weekdays.

do.	Sproughton	......	●		Yes		13	Continuously from 6.0 a.m. Mons.
Bramford	Lime Works	.....	●		Yes	1	23	From { 8.0 a.m. to 10.0 a.m. Daily. / 12.45 p.m. to 2.0 p.m. SX. / 2.0 p.m. to 4.0 p.m. SO. / 6.20 p.m. to 7.15 p.m. / Daily.
Claydon	Station	....	●		Yes	1	50	Continuously ......
Needham	do.	... .	●	Double Line Block.	Yes	3	45	Continuously from 4.0 a.m. Mons.
Stowmarket	Yard	.....	●		Yes	3	17	do. from 4.0 a.m. Mons.
do.	Station	.....	●		...	...	26	Continuously ....

38.   Some sixteen months later, on 21st November 1930, we find that the lane has been diverted under two newly-built bridges, just to the north of the former level crossings. One of the level crossing gates remains, but was later removed as part of the general tidying up of the site. A tank locomotive is standing on the beet factory line, and beyond it a crane is at work in the exchange sidings. In 2015 this rural scene had been transformed into one of industrial and retail development. (J.Richardson collection)

39.   Over the years, several small locomotives were employed on the railway system within the sugar beet factory. This Peckett 0-6-0ST no. 698 *Beatrice* had a long stay, from 1925 until 1957, and here we see it at work in the factory around 1952. (C.Fisher collection)

40. The last steam locomotive to work at the factory was another Peckett 0-6-0ST, no. 2000, which had arrived in 1955. On 17th March 1973 it was taking part in one of the open days held here, when cab loads of railway enthusiasts were able to enjoy footplate rides from the factory to the exchange sidings and back. It was last steamed in 1976, leaving a small diesel shunter in charge until rail traffic ceased in 1982. (C.Fisher)

41. Work is progressing on lifting the beet factory exchange sidings, as a class 105 DMU heads south past Sproughton signalbox on 22nd July 1984. The new A14 dual carriageway is taking shape behind the train, and the concrete arch is the first sign of the road bridge which will span the railway at this point. (S.McNae)

S.P

S.B

S.P

Station

W

W

S.P

S.B

S.P

Station

F.B.

Allotment Garden

F.B.

S.Ps

N

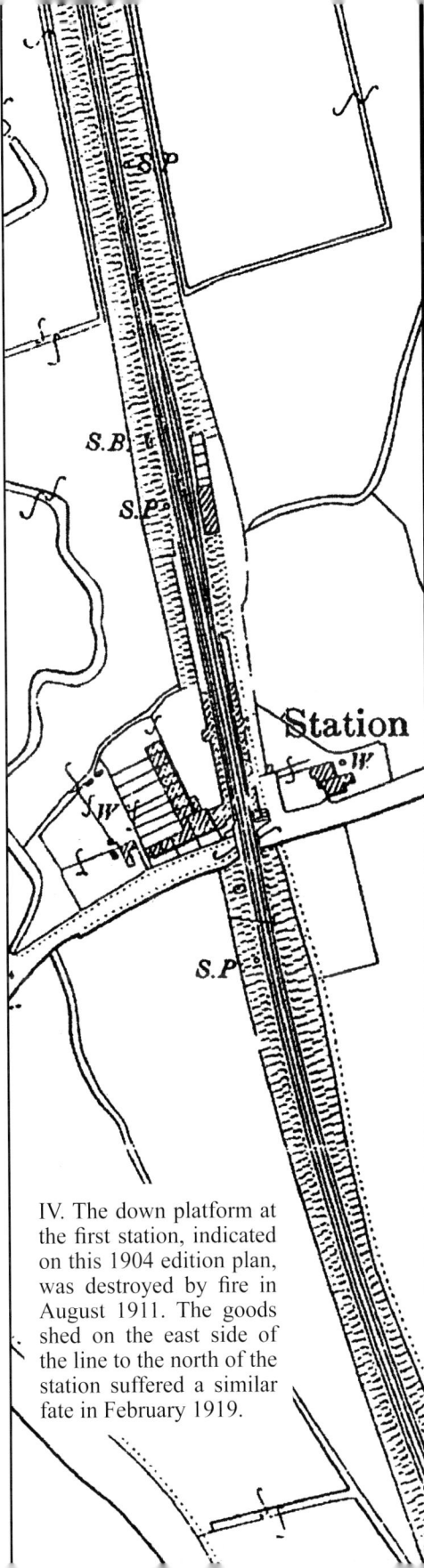

IV. The down platform at the first station, indicated on this 1904 edition plan, was destroyed by fire in August 1911. The goods shed on the east side of the line to the north of the station suffered a similar fate in February 1919.

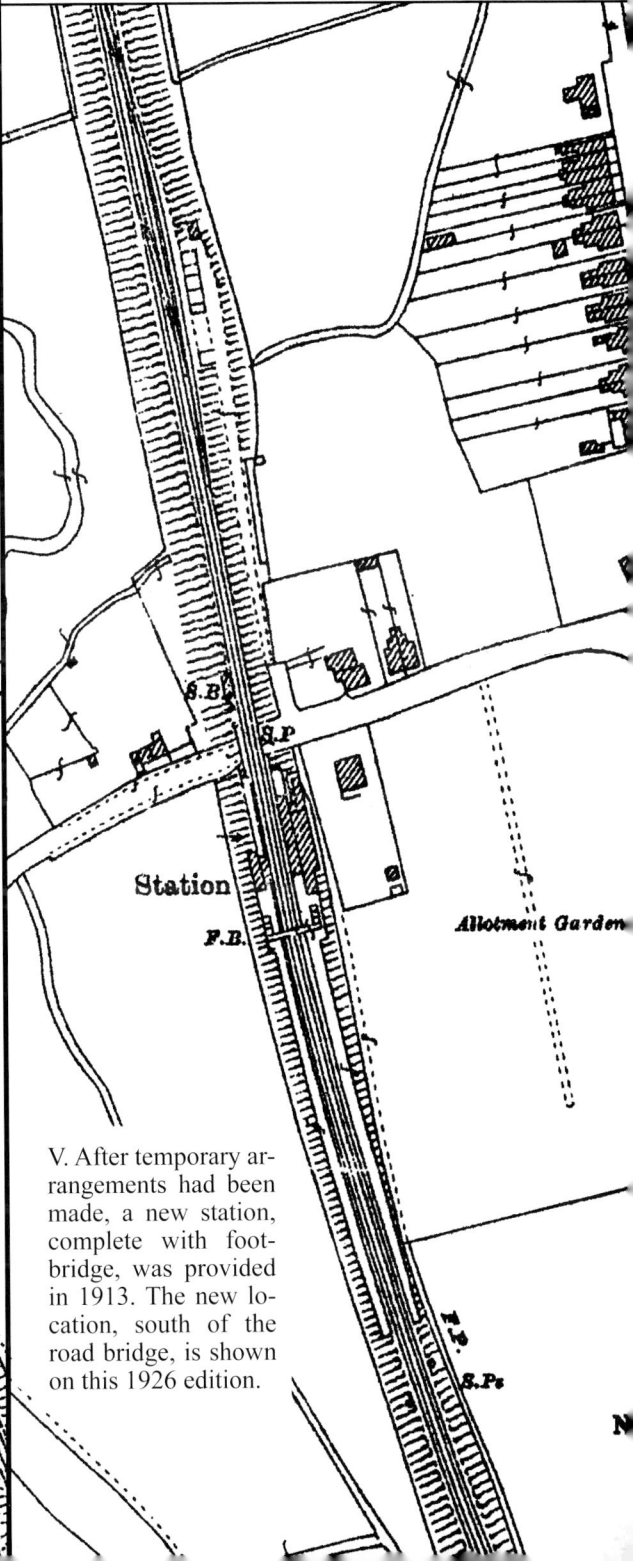

V. After temporary arrangements had been made, a new station, complete with footbridge, was provided in 1913. The new location, south of the road bridge, is shown on this 1926 edition.

42. As we look in a generally eastward direction along a quiet Suffolk lane, the railway merges seamlessly into the scene. The tree and roadside cottages hide some of the detail, but there are wagons to the right of the signalbox, and the steps up to the station can be seen to the left of the bridge, next to the two-storey station building. This image was taken from a card posted in 1910. (D.C.Chappell collection)

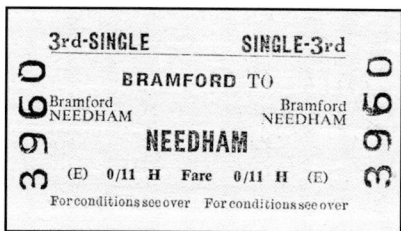

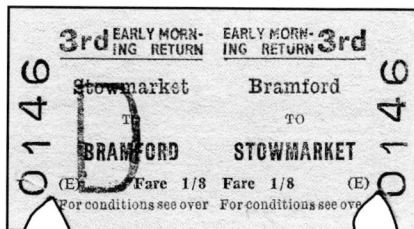

43. The fire on 1st August 1911 resulted in the destruction of the station building, and the subsequent demolition of the platform on which it stood. This was the scene a few days later, looking northwards from a signal post, and we can see that the cottages too had suffered in the blaze, although the up platform and its shelter appear to be unscathed. Opposite the signal box, there are a few wagons on the siding, next to trees which all but shield the goods shed from view. By coincidence, this shed too was destroyed by fire, some eight years later.
(National Railway Museum)

44. Commendably, the Great Eastern wasted no time in restoring train services to the community, quickly building a basic temporary platform immediately south of the road bridge. The photographer's vantage point for our previous picture is immediately beyond the platform.
(National Railway Museum)

GREAT EASTERN RAILWAY This ticket is Issued subject to the Regulations & conditions stated in the Company's Time Tables & Bills.

THIRD CLASS

BRAMFORD to

2518

Via

Fare............s........d

L. N. E. R.
CHEAP DAY
Ipswich
TO
BRAMFORD
Available on day of issue only as per Bills.
THIRD
For conditions see back

L. N. E. R.
CHEAP DAY
Bramford
TO
IPSWICH
Available on day of issue only.
THIRD
For conditions see back

C.D. 1162

4266

IPSWICH

45.   A replacement station on the embankment to the south of the road bridge was authorised in 1912, and at much the same time the signal box seen in picture 43 was replaced by this structure, situated immediately north of the bridge. It was fairly short-lived, and was abolished in 1929, to be replaced by the new signal box at Sproughton. (G.Austin collection)

46.   Class B1 4-6-0 no. 61046 runs into the station with a northbound stopping train during the early 1950s. The gate on the extreme left leads to the stairway down to road level. Passenger services were withdrawn with effect from 2nd May 1955. (Suffolk Record Office, Ipswich, K681/1/59/3)

47. The platforms and buildings were constructed on supports projecting from the embankment, as this picture clearly shows. We are looking eastwards, some years after the station closed. (B.W.L Brooksbank)

G. E. R.

Bramford

48. The disused buildings remained in place for almost exactly a decade after closure but on 30th April 1965 the photographer found a demolition gang hard at work. Balanced precariously on the roof, one of the workmen throws down another piece of material to add to the growing pile of debris on the platform. (D.C.Chappell)

49. Our last look at the location shows the covered staircase up from the road to the station, together with the arches on which the building was supported. A flag dangling from the woodwork warns of the demolition work, again on 30th April 1965. Fifty years later, no trace of the station remained. (D.C.Chappell)

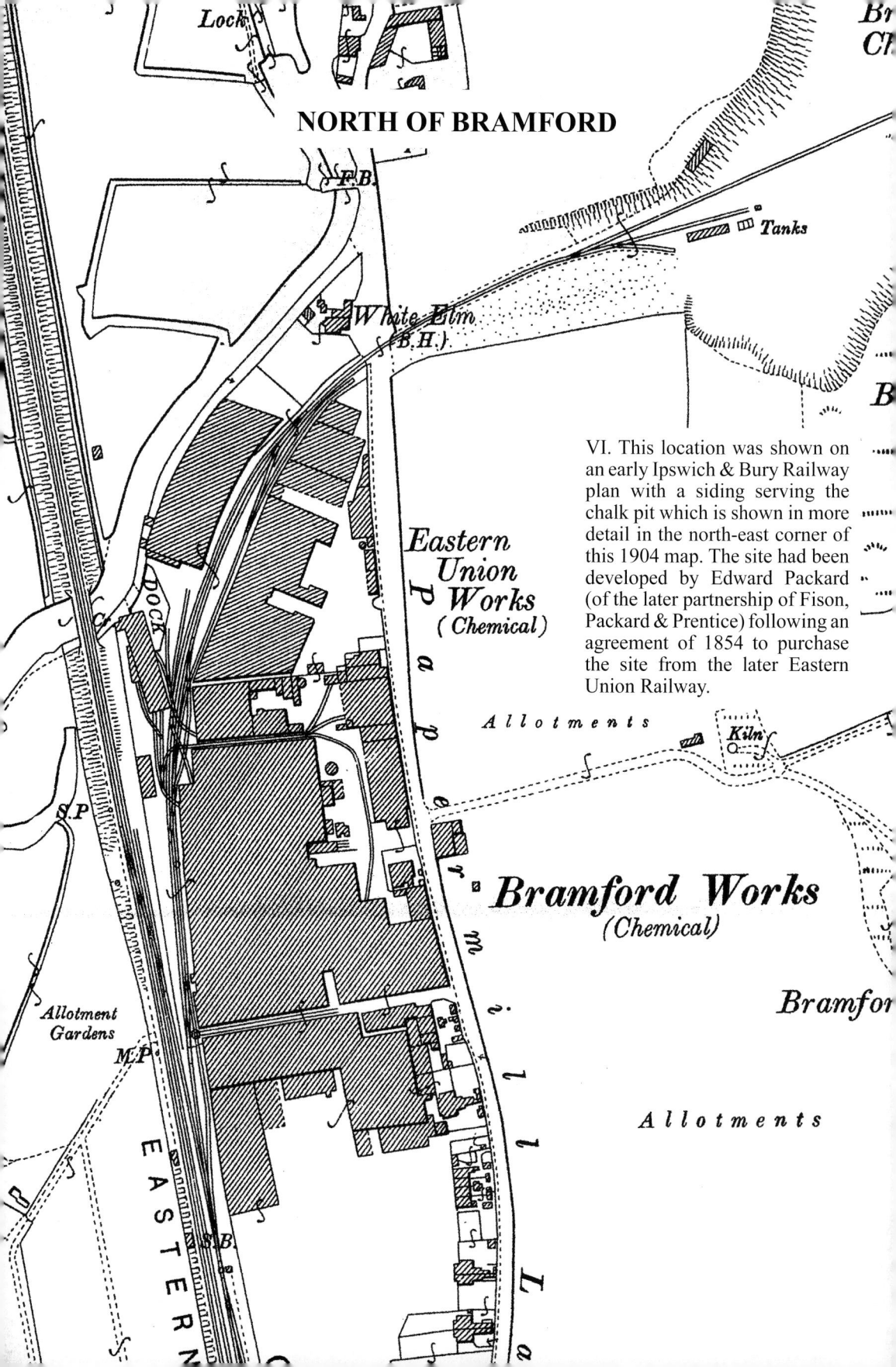

Lock

F.B.

Tanks

White Elm
(B.H.)

Eastern
Union
Works
(Chemical)

VI. This location was shown on an early Ipswich & Bury Railway plan with a siding serving the chalk pit which is shown in more detail in the north-east corner of this 1904 map. The site had been developed by Edward Packard (of the later partnership of Fison, Packard & Prentice) following an agreement of 1854 to purchase the site from the later Eastern Union Railway.

Allotments

Kiln

DOCK

S.P

Paper Mill La

Bramford Works
(Chemical)

Bramfor

Allotment
Gardens

M.P

Allotments

EASTERN

S.B.

50. Here is the industrial complex in 1911, with Lime Works signalbox to the west of the main line. A wagon is standing at the covered loading bay, and in the centre of the picture we can see a siding striking off through the buildings towards the chalk pit. Fisons sold the fertilizer business in 1982, and after a number of changes of ownership, the factory was closed in 2003. Rail traffic had ceased some 35 years earlier, and the signalbox was abolished on 26th June 1968.
(National Railway Museum)

51. As late as February 1991, these tracks embedded in the roadway at the north east corner of the complex provided a reminder of the long-abandoned line through the factory to the chalk pit.
(S.McNae)

CLAYDON

VII. This 1904 edition shows typical station facilities for a small village, located to the east, which in 1851 had a population of 540. Great Blakenham was a smaller community, a similar distance to the west. There is no evidence of any of the industrial businesses which were to follow in the 20th century. The first, and by far the largest, was Mason's Portland Cement plant to the southwest of the level crossing, which was operational with a private siding, by 1912.

S.P.

S.B.

L.B.

Goods Yard

Claydon Station

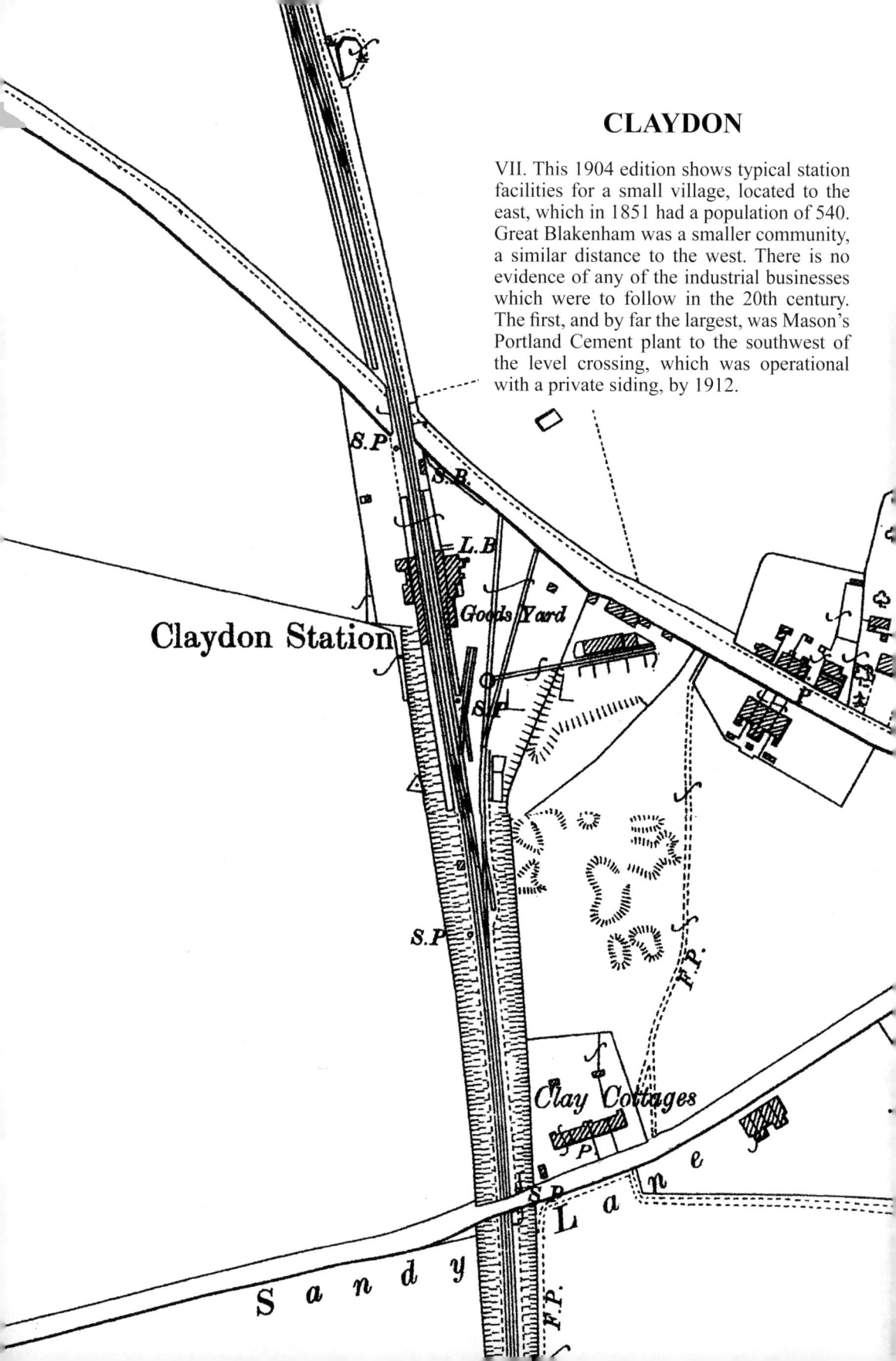

S.P.

S.P.

F.P.

Clay Cottages

P

S.P.

Sandy Lane

F.P.

52. We are looking northwards from the down platform, probably just before the grouping. Both platforms boast substantial wooden shelters of a somewhat ornate design although, even at this date, they look slightly out of place in their workaday surroundings. The sidings to the left form part of the facilities provided for the cement works, while a row of open wagons is standing in the goods yard behind the up platform. (G.Austin collection)

53. Occupying a large area of land to the west of the railway, the cement works dominated the area from the time it was built until demolition in the early 21st century. A former GER 0-6-0 is busy in the down side sidings during the inter-war years. (D.C.Chappell collection)

54.   Class B12 4-6-0 no. 61535 runs into the platform with a down stopping train in the mid-1950s. The shelters had been removed earlier in the decade, leaving both platforms open to the elements and to a constant cloud of cement dust from the works. (H.N.James/M&GN Circle)

55.   As we look southwards over the level crossing gates on 2nd June 1962, the pleasing gable end of the station building can be seen to good advantage. The last passenger train called on 15th June 1962, the goods yard was closed at the end of March 1971, and the neglected station building was controversially demolished in February 1991. (Stations UK)

56.   The cement works continued to generate rail traffic on a regular basis into the 1990s. Sandwiched between coal hoppers and cement wagons, no. 37078 is shunting in the factory siding in 1985. Thirty years later, a housing development covered much of the former factory site (J.Day)

G. E. R.

Claydon

57. Adding to the industrial atmosphere of the area, the Zenith works of the British Steel Piling Company Limited was established to the north-east of the level crossing in 1921. The company's private siding was in use until the early 1970s, and some of the abandoned trackwork remained in place for years afterwards. Beyond the gate marking the limit of the siding, a class 47 heads towards Ipswich along the main line on 28th February 1991. (S.McNae)

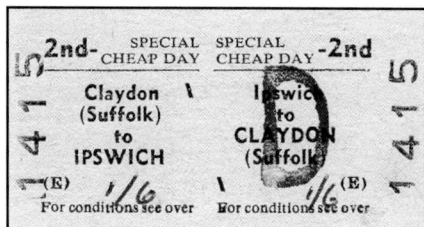

58. During the late 1930s, class B17/5 4-6-0 no. 2870 *City of London* steams through the pretty tree-lined cutting near the village of Baylham with a southbound train. This is one of two locomotives which had been rebuilt to this design in 1937 for use on the prestige "East Anglian" express between Norwich and Liverpool Street. (I.C.Allen/Transport Treasury)

59. During 1980, an aggregates terminal was established on a 4-acre site to the east of the line at Barham, a mile or so north of Claydon, with the aid of a £1m government grant. After trial trips earlier in the month, a regular traffic flow from Westbury began on 15th October that year. Here we see no. 31156 working a test train on 6th June 1986, checking the suitability of the terminal for bogie wagons. The signal controlling movements within the siding is to the right of the locomotive. In 2015 the terminal was being used up to three times a week for unloading trains of aggregate from Mountsorrel in Leicestershire. (J.Day)

NEEDHAM

VIII. The location of the station at the southeast extremity of the town is shown in this 1904 edition map. The route north of the station was confined by the existing High Street properties to the west and the Navigation to the east. The oddly named "Camping Land" adjacent to the gas works dates to medieval times when it was used for the primitive precursor of football, known as "campball".

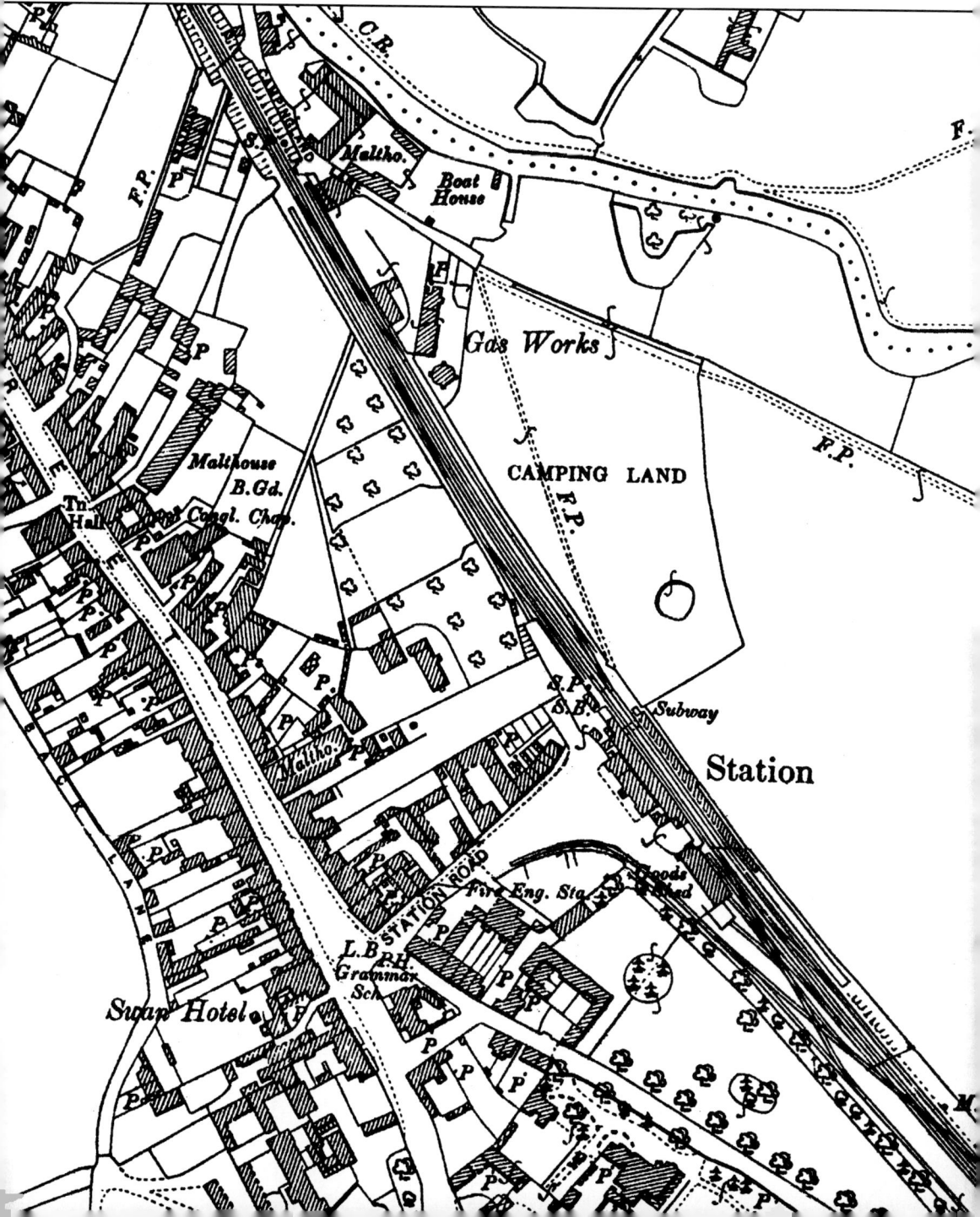

60. Boasting an extravagant array of gables and turrets, the station exterior as originally built was eye-catching, to say the least. It was the work of Ipswich architect Frederick Barnes, who was also responsible for the main buildings at Claydon and Stowmarket. Here it is, in all its splendour, around the beginning of the twentieth century. (Needham Market Society)

61. Having been greeted by the imposing frontage, the average passenger might well have felt a strong sense of anti-climax on reaching the platform. The wooden planked surface adds to a somewhat gloomy scene under the canopy, again around 1900. An express train is approaching from the north, with the buildings of the town gasworks to the right of it. Neither will do anything to enhance the atmosphere of the place. (J. Watling collection)

62. In earlier days, waiting passengers on the eastern platform had been protected from the weather by a shelter similar to those at Claydon and Bramford, which covered most of the length of the platform. This had disappeared by the time of our 1920s photograph, having been replaced by this building which provided waiting and toilet facilities. At the far end of the platform is the entrance to the subway, a feature rarely found at country stations in East Anglia. (G.Austin collection)

63. Now we are looking northwards on the same day. There are a few cattle wagons in the siding beyond the signal box, while part of the goods shed creeps into the picture on the left. By this time, changes had been made to the main building too, as we shall see in more detail later. (G.Austin collection)

64. Two track workers step back as class B12 4-6-0 no. 61533 passes the signal box, heading for Ipswich with a passenger train during the 1950s. (R.K.Blencowe collection)

65. It is interesting to compare this 1960s picture of the western elevation of the main building with that shown in picture 60. Gone are the turrets and curved gable ends, which have been replaced by castellated towers and angular gables, but the frontage is still impressive. Photographic evidence suggests that this work had been undertaken in the early 1920s. (B.D.J.Walsh/GERS)

CLASS TYPE	FARE PAID
2S	9 P

British Rail

NEEDHAM MARKET

to

STOWMARKET

ISSUED SUBJECT TO THE REGULATIONS AND CONDITIONS IN THE PUBLICATIONS AND NOTICES OF THE BRITISH RAILWAYS BOARD

NOT TRANSFERABLE

BR4392/1

RE-OPENING OF NEEDHAM MARKET

ISSUING OFFICE

PAYTRAIN

FIRST DAY OF TRAVEL SUPPLEMENTARY SOUVENIR TICKET

DATE OF ISSUE   TICKET No.

6 Dec. 71   0332

66. From the railway side though, the prospect remained unattractive into the 1960s. Patched up brickwork makes the subway entrance look uninviting, while after dark the gas lamp would add an old time atmosphere, but give precious little illumination. Only the totem sign is in any way modern. The station was closed to passenger traffic from 2nd January 1967, not long after this picture was taken. (B.D.J.Walsh/GERS)

67. Less than five years later, on 6th December 1971, the station was reopened as an unstaffed halt named "Needham Market", since when the only trains to call have been local services running over the Bury St Edmunds line. The revised name is prominent as a class 47 races past with an up express in the early 1970s. After years of neglect, the Grade 2 listed station building was the subject of an award-winning restoration project completed in 2002. (I.C.Allen/Transport Treasury)

Allotment Gardens

Uplands

Hill **STOWMARKET**

Black Barn

Spoonman's Farm

Mell

FP

STOWMARKET U D

Church

Sta

Cb

STOWMARKET

Sheepcote Hall

Reservoir (Disused)

Sewage Farm (Stowmarket U D & East Stow R D Joint Councils)

FP

FP

FP

FP

CALIFORNIA

Allot. Gdns.

Silk Factory

Reservoir (Disused)

F.B.

F.B.

Ford age a F.B.

Gdns.

Allot.

Weir

Lock (Disused)

RAILWAY

New Britannic Chemical Works

F.B.

Allot. Gdns.

Cresby

COMBS FORD

Stowmarket 1
Ipswich 11 } M.S.

School

F.P.

P.U.

Silk Wo (Dis)

IX. This 1928 edition map at a scale of 6 ins. to 1 mile, together with the accompanying aerial photograph, indicates the level of industrial activity that had developed in a small market town, resulting in a population growth of about 50% since the opening of the railway some 80 years earlier.

68.   We are looking south from the level crossing on 10th September 1911, with the short platforms and covered footbridge readily apparent. Over to the left, behind the up platform, an old coach body serves as some kind of store, while the motley assortment of buildings are all rail-connected. Three tall chimneys are also indicative of the industrial nature of the area around the railway. The flower bed and neatly-tended border at the north end of the platform appear somewhat incongruous in these surroundings. (GERS/Windwood collection)

69.   In Great Eastern days, this wooden shed provided covered trans-shipment facilities in the large goods yard. Here is the shed in the early 1920s, with two horse drawn carts waiting outside, only a matter of yards from the main line tracks. The yard crane, with its distinctive conical roof, is further to the left. (G.Austin collection)

70. Further covered accommodation was provided by this open fronted wooden structure serving a siding which terminated at the south end of the platform ramp. The dilapidated building, seemingly supported by baulks of timber, contrasts with the imposing southern end of the station next to it. (G.Austin collection)

71. In view of our two previous pictures, it is not surprising that one of the first tasks of the newly-formed LNER was to construct a modern goods shed, more befitting a thriving country town. This is the new building under construction during the mid 1920s, with the north wall and roof complete. The attention to detail revealed by the circumflex accent over the last "O" in the lettering is noteworthy. (G.Austin collection)

72. This picture, dated 9th October 1928, shows the considerable industrial development which took place alongside the railway to the south of the station over the years. As we look northwards, there are five separate industrial concerns to be seen, whose products ranged from artificial silk to fertiliser and explosives - a surprisingly wide spread of industries in a basically agricultural area. Each had its own network of railway sidings, and a new signal box, Stowmarket Works, was installed hereabouts in 1941 to help deal with the traffic in this area. It was taken out of use in October 1957. (© English Heritage. Licensor www.rcahms.gov.uk)

73.   Class K3 2-6-0 no. 61989 runs into the station with an up stopping train on 28th May 1953. The footbridge beyond the level crossing enabled pedestrians to cross the railway on the frequent occasions that the gates barred their way on the busy Stowupland Road. (R.E.Vincent/Transport Treasury)

74.   There is no sign of activity on the platforms, as class B1 4-6-0 no. 61228 heads north with a down express train on 3rd August 1956. The footbridge seen here was replaced prior to electrification and was moved to a new home at Weybourne, on the North Norfolk Railway. (R.K.Blencowe collection)

75. Overlooked by Stowmarket Yard signalbox, class J67 0-6-0T no. 68518 shunts wagons in the extensive goods sidings to the south of the station during the 1950s. A shunting engine, latterly a 204 hp diesel, was stationed here until well into the following decade. (I.C.Allen/Transport Treasury)

76. Other private sidings existed to the north of the station, although the premises they served had a far more rural air than the factories along the Gipping Valley. We are looking north from the footbridge next to the level crossing in July 1966, and can see two gated private sidings curving away to the east. Brewers Sutton & Phillips Ltd owned the nearer one, whilst the other had been provided for W.R.Hewitt, a timber merchant, in 1904. The siding on the left crossed the main road diagonally on the level before swinging westwards to terminate by the river bank. (S.Moore)

77. A few years later, we see major track alterations taking place to the north of the station. The down main line has been replaced with concrete-sleepered track and the crossover has been removed, while the sidings have been disconnected and most of their rails lifted. (D.C.Pearce collection)

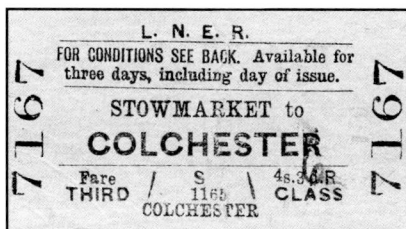

78. Much of the traditional atmosphere remained when this picture was taken on 12th June 1969. The length of the down platform, restricted by the points leading to the goods yard, had become something of an embarrassment as train lengths increased. At this time, operating instructions ordained that all passenger trains exceeding five vehicles in length should stop with the rearmost five coaches at the platform. (British Railways)

79. A varied selection of motor vehicles occupies the area in front of the station, again on 12th June 1969. The building looks well maintained, with a "British Rail" sign over the entrance to the booking hall. (British Railways)

80. By the 21st century, extensions to the platform and to the car parking facilities had all but covered the area of the former goods yard. Only two tracks remained in 2015, and these had become a centre for Direct Rail Services operations in the area. This is particularly busy in late Autumn and early Winter, when the Rail Head Treatment trains are performing their leaf-clearing activities. Here we are looking southwards on 5th October 2012, with seven class 57 locomotives and the purpose-built wagons awaiting deployment on these duties. (B.Steele)

81. The lengthened platforms are clearly seen as no. 90005 slows for the station stop on 15th April 2015 with a Norwich to Liverpool Street train. Much of the former railway and industrial land to both east and west of the line is given over to car parking. (R.J.Adderson)

HAUGHLEY

*Haughley
Junction*

S.B.

Railway in course of construction

M.P.

S.P.

S.

Post *Railway Tavern*
(P.H.)

C.R.

S.P.

S.B. **Haughley
Station**

EASTERN UNION LINE

G.E.R.

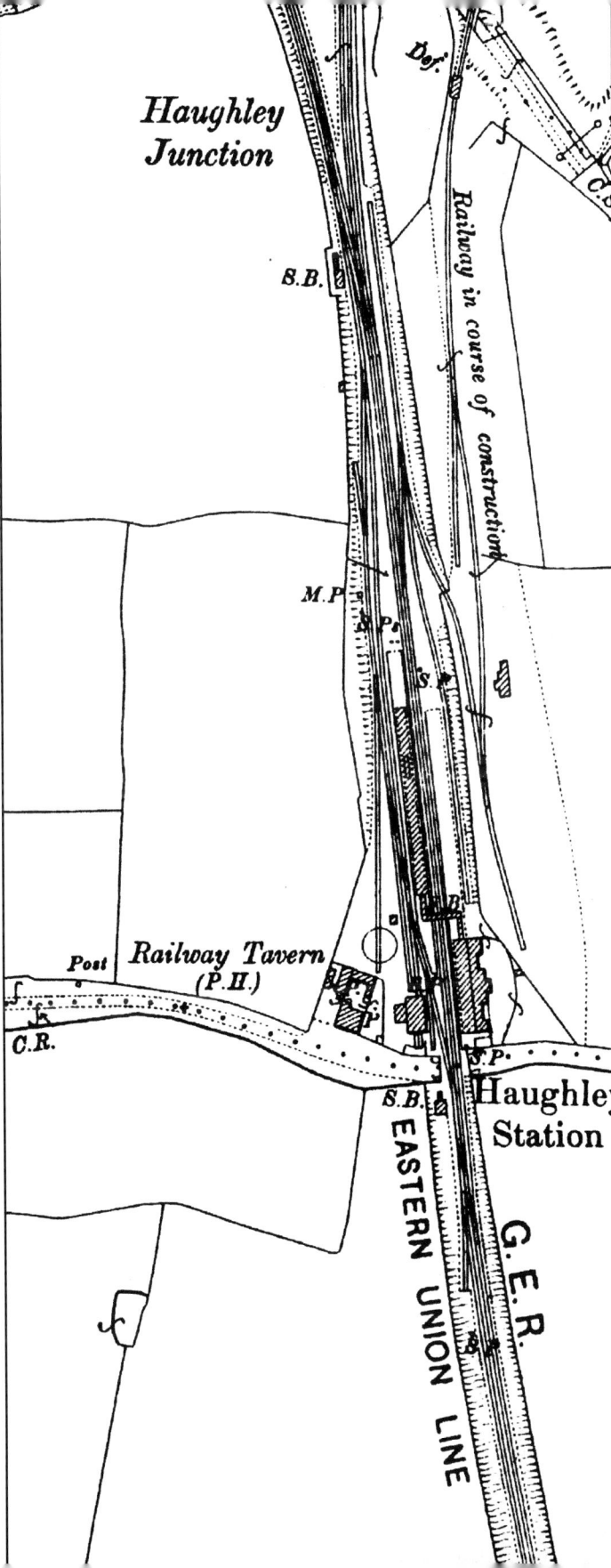

X. The original 1846 station serving the village of Haughley, and known as Haughley Road, was located on the line to Bury St. Edmunds about one mile to the west of what, in 1849, became the junction for the route to Norwich. The new station was known at various times as Haughley, Haughley Road and Haughley West. The last of these names was used following the opening of the Mid-Suffolk Light Railway, shown on this 1904 map "in course of construction". Until 1939 the light railway had its own station to the east of the main line.

82. The station building had none of the architectural extravagances of those further south, possibly because it was built a few years later, but nonetheless presented an air of solid Victorian prosperity. Towards the end of the Great Eastern era, a horse and cart wait by the entrance porch while their owner goes about his business at the station. (G.Austin collection)

83. This is the signal box which stood immediately south-west of the level crossing, again in the early 1920s. Following track alterations in the station area, it was closed in 1933, leaving its counterpart at the junction to regulate train workings here until 1971. (G.Austin collection)

84.   Class J15 0-6-0 no. 65447 has arrived in the bay platform with two vintage six-wheel coaches and a van forming the 1.45 pm from Laxfield on 24th July 1951. This was one of the two daily trains in each direction over the former Mid-Suffolk Light Railway which ran across the agricultural heartland of the county to the little town of Laxfield. It closed on 26th July 1952, after a working life of just fifty years. In the distance, beyond the signal box, the line to Bury St Edmunds leaves the Norwich route and curves away to the west. (G.Powell/GERS)

85.   We are looking out from the Junction signalbox as class J17 0-6-0 no. 65553 heads north with a long goods train, which is signalled for the Norwich line. The silo in the background stands on the site of the Mid-Suffolk Railway's original terminus, which had been taken out of use in 1939, some fifteen years before the date of this picture. (I.C.Allen/Transport Treasury)

86. In the early hours of an October morning in 1955, a goods train from March was unable to stop on the downhill gradient approaching the station, and was derailed at the catch points by the level crossing. This was the scene as "clearing up" operations got underway, with two steam cranes in attendance, and class K3 2-6-0 no. 61801 surrounded by the wreckage of its train. (MSLR Archive)

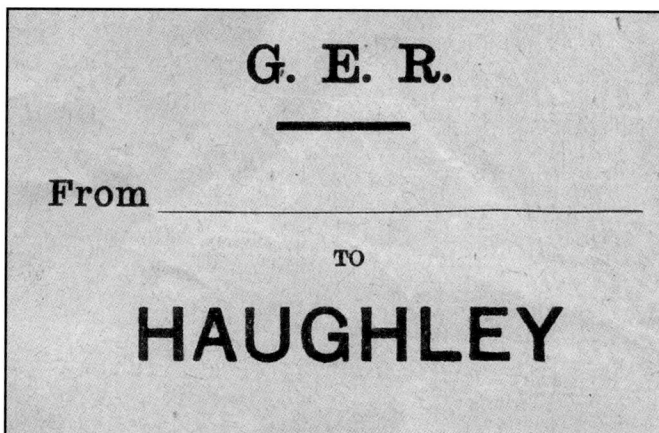

G. E. R.
————
From _____
TO
HAUGHLEY

87. Still quite new, a Brush type 2 diesel speeds down the gradient towards the station with a Norwich to Liverpool Street express in the late 1950s. The Bury St Edmunds line goes off to the left of the picture, while the Mid-Suffolk still curves away to the right. Appearances are deceptive though, for the Laxfield line had been lifted soon after closure, except for this short section which was retained as a shunt spur for the goods yard until 31st May 1963.
(I.C.Allen/Transport Treasury)

2nd-SINGLE SINGLE-2nd
Haughley to
Haughley   Haughley
Finningham   Finningham
FINNINGHAM
0452   0452
(E)   1/2   Fare   1/2   (E)
For conditions see over   For conditions see over

PLATFORM. ADMIT ONE
FINNINGHAM
This ticket is issued on condition that
the Company will not be liable
to the holder for any injury
or loss, personal or otherwise,
however caused.
L.N.E.R.   5156
1 D. A

88.   There are no signs of life, as class B12 4-6-0 no. 61567 calls with a stopping train for Ipswich on 3rd May 1958. The station was perhaps at its busiest in the early hours of the morning, when a series of complex shunting movements took place to exchange vehicles between the mail trains to and from Peterborough, Norwich and Liverpool Street. This nightly operation continued into the late 1960s. (R.C.Riley/Transport Treasury)

89.   An overall view of the station on the evening of 22nd May 1966 emphasises the semi-circular profiles of the canopies, although comparison with earlier pictures will reveal that the one on the down platform has been drastically reduced in length. The last passenger train called on 31st December 1966, and the platforms and buildings were subsequently demolished. (S.Moore)

FINNINGHAM

XI. The choice of name for this station which was actually located in the parish of Bacton is something of a mystery, given the fact that the population of Bacton was somewhat higher than that of Finningham. The TRAMWAY shown to the south of the station on this 1904 map amounted to little more than a lengthy siding, possibly flush with the surface of a roadway. It is likely that it was used at various times by a number of local corn merchants in view of the fact that, on an earlier map, the building adjacent to the main road is marked as a granary.

e

Finningham Station

F.P.

Post

S.P

Def.

R.P.   *F.B.*
W
L.B
F.W

Goods Shed   *F.P*   *F.W*

S.P

Railway Tavern

W

Cattle Pens

4 ft. R.H.

S.P.

F.P.   *G.P.*

Smith

TRAMWAY

F.P

R.H.
W

90. The bridge spanning the tracks at the north end of the station provides an overall view of the location as it was in the early years of the twentieth century. A goods train, including two rail-mounted cranes, is making its way towards Stowmarket. Beyond the footbridge, the station building obscures the goods shed and yard, but to the west of the line we have a clear view of the large rail-served premises of corn merchants Quintons, with its multi-sided office building. (G.L.Kenworthy collection)

91. Here is the south end of the station on 1st July 1911, with a number of wagons in the small yard to the west. On the opposite side of the main line, a siding leads into the timber goods shed, which provides further facilities for handling the area's freight traffic. (HMRS/H.F.Hilton collection, ref ABB401)

92. A wagon turntable on the line into the goods shed gave access to another siding, which headed eastwards at a 90 degree angle from the running lines. In a very short distance, this siding served a loading dock, cattle pens and the coal yard. This was the scene, again on 1st July 1911, with the office belonging to Moy, the coal merchant, by the yard gate in the distance. (HMRS/H.F.Hilton collection, ref ABB336)

93. Hauling a lightweight goods train, class J17 0-6-0 no. 65542 stands in the shadow of the platform awning on 28th May 1958. This Norwich based engine, together with the angle of the sun, suggests that the train is the pick-up goods which, for most of the decade, was scheduled to leave Norwich around 3.20 a.m. and to arrive at Stowmarket some 9½ hours later, with time allowed for shunting at all the goods yards en route. (Milepost 92½)

94. By contrast, "Britannia" 4-6-2 no. 70038 *Robin Hood* speeds through the station with a Norwich to Liverpool Street express train on the same day. (Milepost 92½)

95. The late afternoon sunshine lights up the main building on 22nd May 1966. It had just reached its centenary, as temporary facilities had been provided when the line first opened, and the contract for this new building had not been awarded until 1865. (S. Moore)

96. This view was taken from a train as it slowed for the station stop, and signs of the final decline are all too evident. Goods facilities had been withdrawn at the end of 1964, the sidings were lifted the following year, and now only a few courses of brickwork and the exposed loading platform show where the goods shed had stood. Just one passenger is waiting for the train, although the well filled bicycle shed suggests that other services may have been better patronised. The last passenger train called here on 5th November 1966. (B.D.J.Walsh/GERS)

97. No. 47634 *Henry Ford* powers past the overgrown remains of the platform, underneath the overhead electrical equipment, with a Liverpool Street to Norwich express on 9th May 1987. Two days later, the full electric timetable came into force on the Great Eastern main line. The signal box had been abolished in June 1968, and now the station building is the only reminder of what used to be. Perhaps surprisingly, this was still standing in 2015. (R.J.Adderson)

Kiln

Swattes
Brick W

F.P.

F.B.

G.E.R.

EASTERN UNION LINE

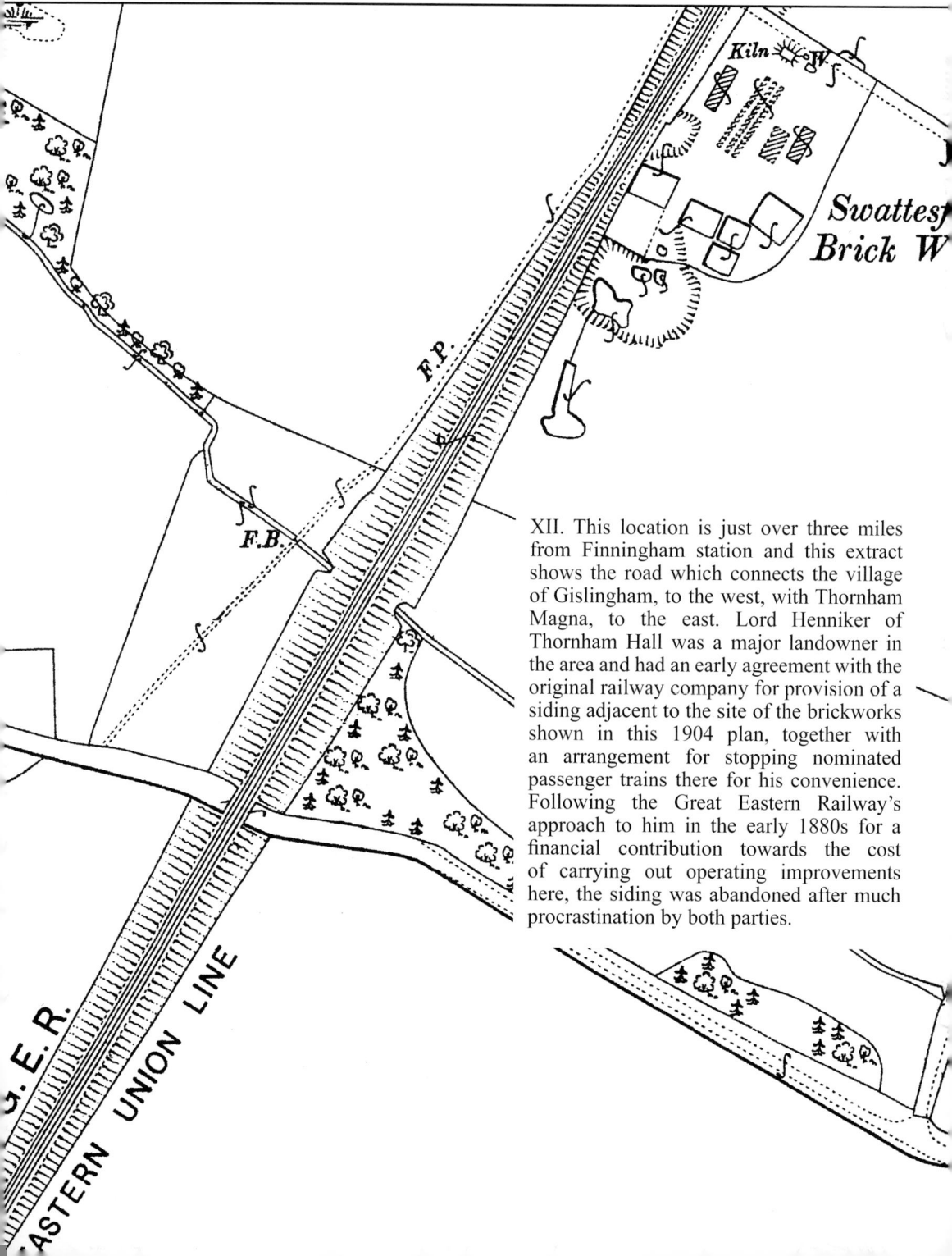

XII. This location is just over three miles from Finningham station and this extract shows the road which connects the village of Gislingham, to the west, with Thornham Magna, to the east. Lord Henniker of Thornham Hall was a major landowner in the area and had an early agreement with the original railway company for provision of a siding adjacent to the site of the brickworks shown in this 1904 plan, together with an arrangement for stopping nominated passenger trains there for his convenience. Following the Great Eastern Railway's approach to him in the early 1880s for a financial contribution towards the cost of carrying out operating improvements here, the siding was abandoned after much procrastination by both parties.

MELLIS

White House

S.P

P.O

F.B.

Old Pound

Corn Mill

G

Memorial Hut

Railway Hotel

Mellis

S.P

P.H

G.P

Cattle
Pens

Malthouse

S.P

S.P

Sta.

S.B.

Corn Mill

U.M.
Chapel

Goods
Shed

S.Ps

W

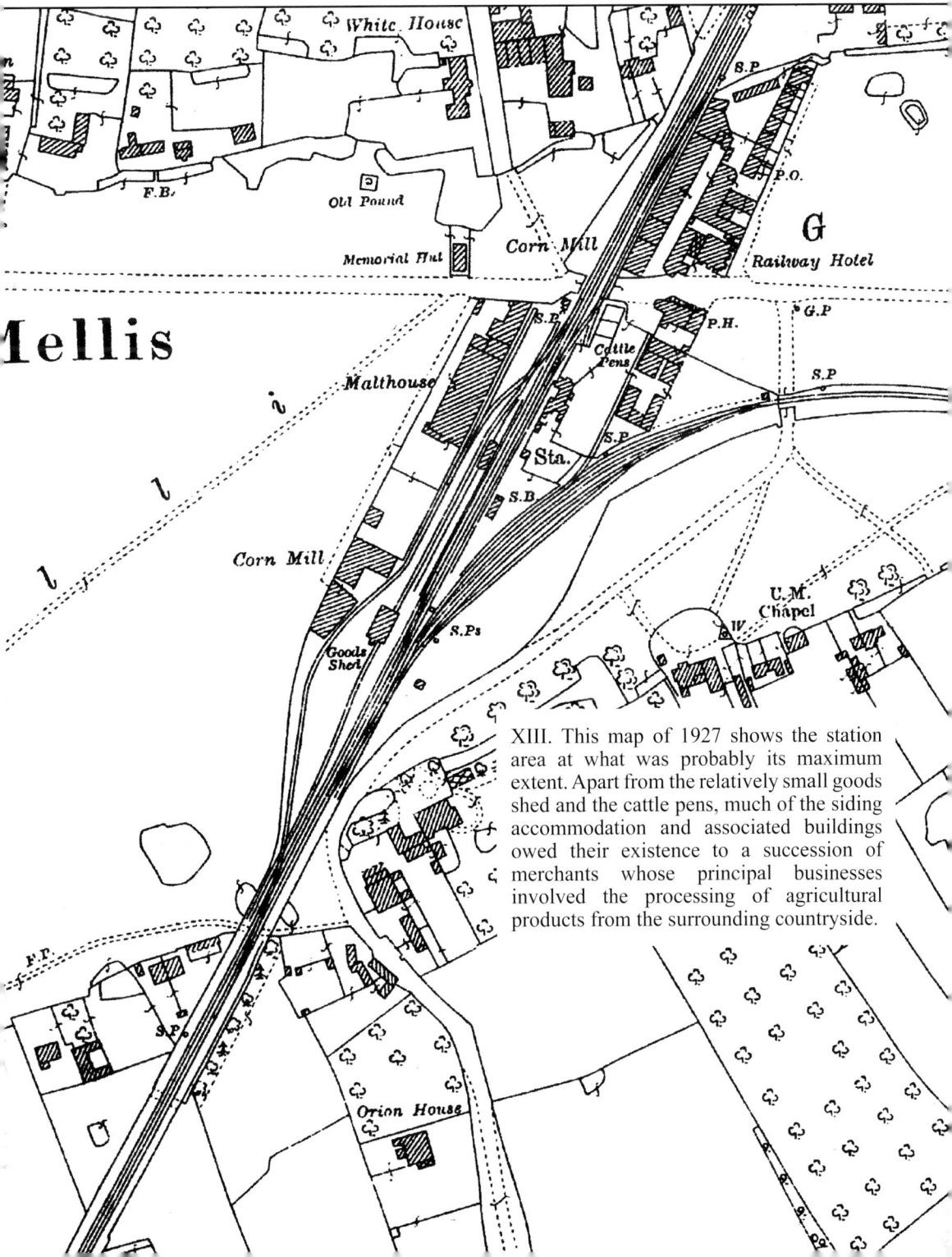

XIII. This map of 1927 shows the station area at what was probably its maximum extent. Apart from the relatively small goods shed and the cattle pens, much of the siding accommodation and associated buildings owed their existence to a succession of merchants whose principal businesses involved the processing of agricultural products from the surrounding countryside.

F.P.

S.P

Orion House

98. We are looking north towards the station during the early years of the twentieth century. A stopping train waits to resume its journey towards Ipswich, while the connection for Eye stands in the branch platform. The maltings buildings behind the down platform are typical of the rural industries which were often attracted by the coming of the railway. (Mellis History Group)

99. A small goods shed was provided behind the down platform, and here we see it during the 1920s, when working horses were still a common sight. (G.Austin collection)

100. An unusual event took place on 9th February 1957, when the station hosted a special train run for the benefit of the Suffolk Hunt. This had originated at Bury St Edmunds and according to a contemporary report conveyed "thirteen handsome horses and 18½ couple of hounds" as well as the huntsmen and followers. Three more horses and riders boarded en route at Elmswell. Here we see a huntsman leading several of the hounds across the boarded crossing at the south end of the platforms. (R.Powell collection)

101. The train used the branch platform, and consisted of ten vans for the animals, with a passenger coach at each end. Class D16/3 4-4-0 no. 62615 is about to leave on the return journey to Elmswell, where it will pick up the hunt participants before returning them to Bury St Edmunds. (I.C.Allen/Transport Treasury)

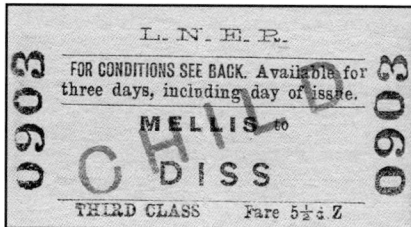

L.N.E.R.
FOR CONDITIONS SEE BACK. Available for
three days, including day of issue.
MELLIS to
DISS
0903   0903
THIRD CLASS   Fare 5½d Z

2nd-SINGLE SINGLE-2nd
Mellis to
Mellis   Mellis
Finningham   Finningham
FINNINGHAM
(E)   1/3   Fare   1/3   (E)
For conditions see over   For conditions see over
2236   2236

102. After our look at the "once off" Hunt special, the next three pictures all depict everyday scenes during the late 1950s. Here, class J17 0-6-0 no. 65542 waits with the goods train from Eye as a DMU heads up the main line. This branch working was part of the itinerary of the early morning Norwich to Stowmarket train seen in picture 93. (I.C.Allen/Transport Treasury)

103. The branch platform still appears to be well maintained, even though the Eye passenger service had been withdrawn over 25 years earlier. A Britannia pacific disturbs the peace as it races northwards with a Liverpool Street to Norwich express. (Milepost 92½)

104. A Metro Cammell DMU resumes its journey southwards after making the station stop on a Norwich to Ipswich train. By this time, diesel railcars such as this operated most of the stopping services, typically taking around 80 minutes for the 46 mile journey, with eleven intermediate stops. (Milepost 92½)

105. Here is the well-maintained station building, seen from the forecourt on 4th July 1965. Goods traffic had ceased from 28th December 1964 and closure to passengers came on 5th November 1966, the last train to call being the 10.52 p.m. from Norwich to Ipswich, which was due here at 11.31 p.m. (J.Watling)

106. We are looking north towards the level crossing from underneath the awning of the down platform shelter on 22nd May 1966. The Barley Merchants' premises beyond the crossing were rail –served for many years, but by now the siding had been lifted. (S.Moore)

107. Following the withdrawal of passenger services, the signal box remained in use for another twenty years. A photographer is preparing for action as no. 47585 *County of Cambridgeshire* approaches the overgrown platforms with a train from Liverpool Street on 29th June 1985. The overhead equipment has been installed, ready for the impending electrification, and by September 1986 the station site had been cleared, following the abolition of the signal box in June 1986. (R.J.Adderson)

2. Eye Branch

YAXLEY HALT

XIV. Although there is no indication of the halt on this 1928 map, it had been opened in December 1922 immediately to the west of the main road, which passed over the bridge. Access from the section of the village north of the railway was by the steps indicated in the road embankment opposite the buildings identified as the Guildhall, but they had probably been provided when the branch opened.

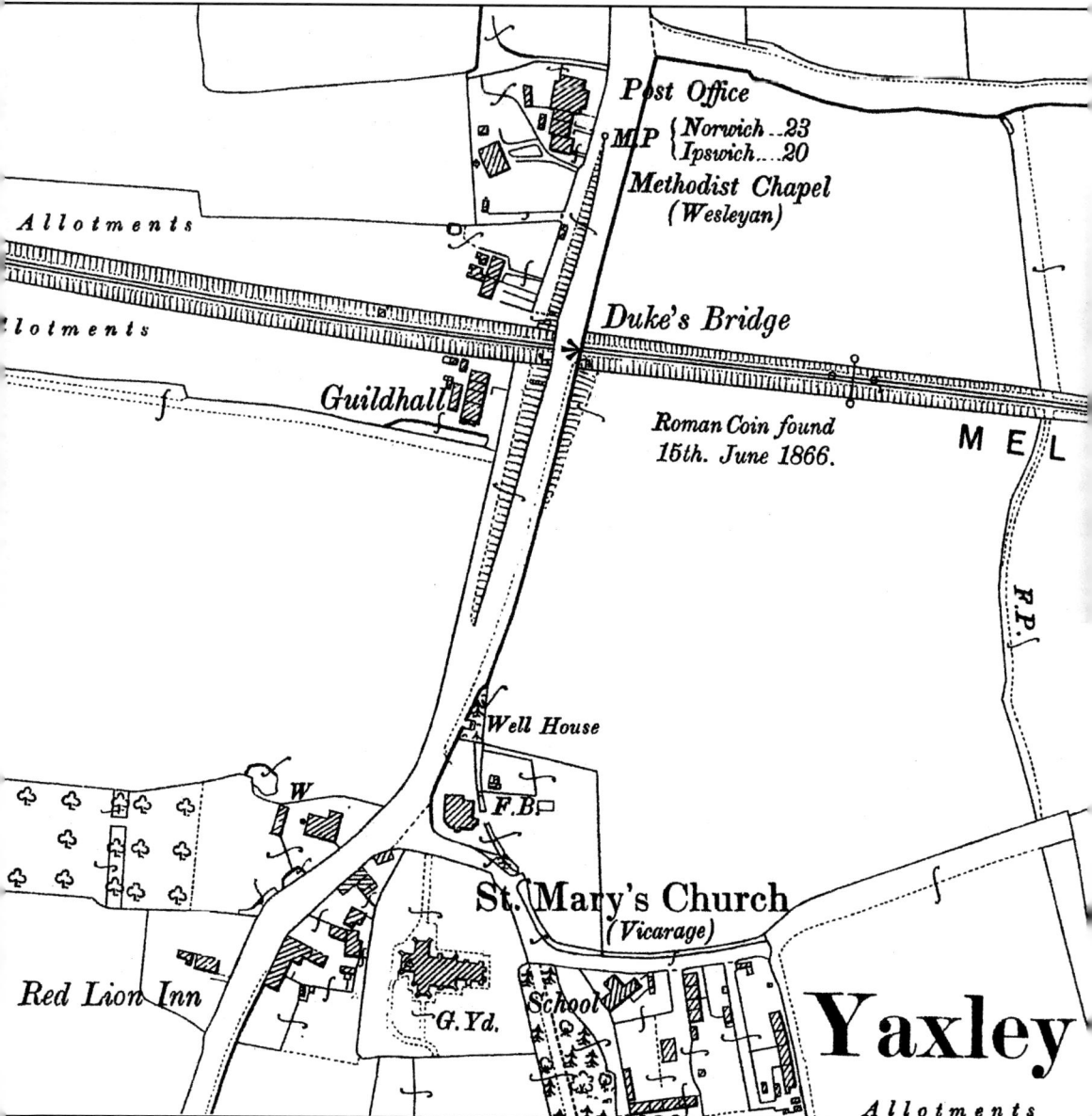

Post Office

M P { Norwich ...23
{ Ipswich 20

Methodist Chapel
(Wesleyan)

Allotments

llotments

Duke's Bridge

Guildhall

Roman Coin found
15th. June 1866.

M E L

F.P.

Well House

W

F.B.

St. Mary's Church
(Vicarage)

Red Lion Inn

G.Yd.

School

Yaxley

Allotments

108. The basic facilities here comprised a short ground-level platform, a lamp and a nameboard, approached by steps down from the road. Not surprisingly, nothing remained at rail level when the photographer visited the site in April 1969, but the bridge, steps and fragments of unmistakably "railway" fencing could still be seen. (S.Moore)

GREAT EASTERN RAILWAY.
issued subject to Regulations in the Company's Time Tables.

EYE to

EYE   EYE

DISS

DISS   DISS

6½d   Fare   6½d

Third Class

8237   8237

Yaxley Halt

Stowmarket to

Yaxley Halt to

Stowmarket

This Ticket is issued subject to the published Conditions and Regulations of the Company. It is available for ONE RETURN JOURNEY ONLY. MARKET TICKET.

THIRD RETURN FARE. 2/2D.

Chandos Lodge

EYE

F.P.

Institu

F.P.

S.P.

Allotment
Gardens
Brewery

Malthouse

S.B.

Goods Shed

Station

Hospital
(Site of)

W

Engine Shed

L.B.

Cattle Pens

Smithy

Cattle Pens

Auction Mart

Pound

MAGDALEN STREET

Gas Works

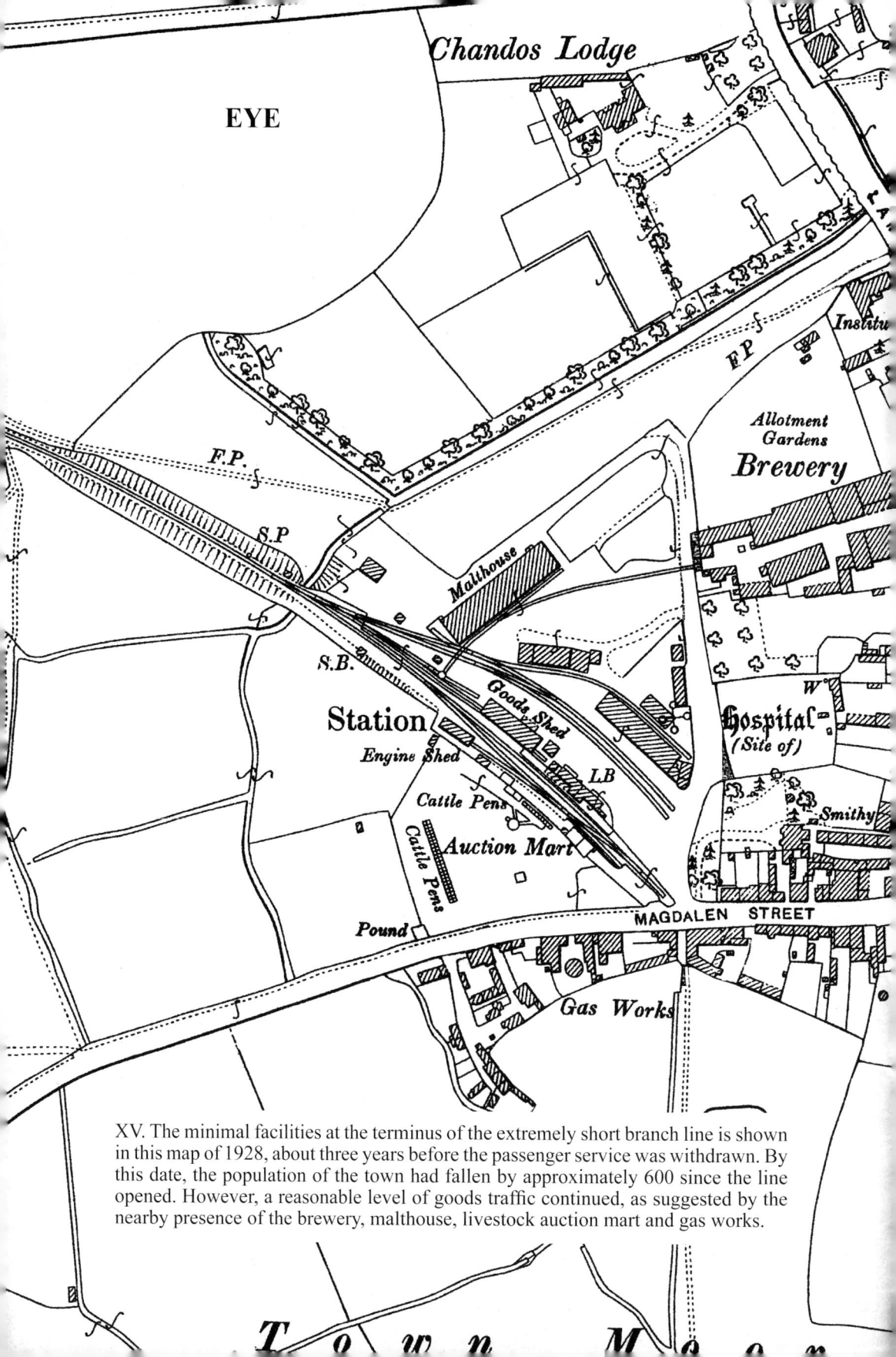

XV. The minimal facilities at the terminus of the extremely short branch line is shown
in this map of 1928, about three years before the passenger service was withdrawn. By
this date, the population of the town had fallen by approximately 600 since the line
opened. However, a reasonable level of goods traffic continued, as suggested by the
nearby presence of the brewery, malthouse, livestock auction mart and gas works.

Town Moor

109. We start our look at the terminus with four photographs dating back to the 1920s. This is the view from the forecourt, with the station building to the left and the goods office and goods shed beyond. (G.Austin collection)

110. Here is the single platform, looking towards Mellis, with a variety of advertising signs covering much of the available brickwork. Two six-wheel coaches await their next round trip to the junction, and milk churns are much in evidence. The wagons in the goods siding over to the right include an example from the Great Western Railway. (G.Austin collection)

111. The single road engine shed was used to stable the branch locomotive overnight. It therefore served no purpose after the passenger services ceased, and was demolished at an unknown date soon afterwards. Certainly it had gone by 1937, although the adjoining water tank was still there in the 1960s. (G.Austin collection)

From 1867 Bradshaw Guide.

267.—MELLIS AND EYE.

Incorporated by 28 and 29 Vic., cap. 249 (5th July, 1865), to construct a line from the Great Eastern at Mellis to Eye. Length, 3 miles. Capital, 15,000*l.* in shares, and 5,000*l.* on loan. Arrangements with Great Eastern.

CAPITAL.—The receipts to 13th August were 7,066*l.*, and the expenditure 6,703*l.*, leaving a balance of 363*l.*

No. of Directors—6; quorum, 3. *Qualification*, 100*l.*

DIRECTORS:

Sir Edward Clarence Kerrison, Bart., M.P., 140, Piccadilly, W.
Lord Henniker, 6, Grafton Street, Bond Street, W.

Edgar Chenery, Esq.
Benjamin Cotton Etteridge, Esq.
Major the Hon. J. M. Henniker, M.P.
Robert Chase, Esq.

112. We are now looking towards the station with the engine shed in the centre of the picture and the lines into to the goods yard fanning out to the north. Unusually, the yard is fenced off from the running lines and is also protected by a gate which is open to rail traffic on this occasion. The small signal box completes the scene. This was converted to a ground frame in 1931 and was abolished in 1943. (G.Austin collection)

113. Class J17 0-6-0 no. 65542 is shunting in the goods yard on an unknown date in the mid-1950s. Several wagons, mostly fairly old wooden-bodied examples, occupy the yard, suggesting that traffic was reasonably buoyant at that time. (I.C.Allen/Transport Treasury)

114. After a break of twenty-five years, a passenger train returned to the branch on 8th September 1956, with the visit of a railtour organised by the Norfolk Railway Society. The goods shed and former passenger station provide the backdrop, as class E4 2-4-0 no. 62797 runs round the train. Later that month, the R.E.C. "Suffolk Venturer" railtour also covered the branch, but there were no further passenger workings after this little flurry of activity. (W.J.Naunton)

115. Not a lot has changed in the early 1960s, some thirty years after passenger services ceased. During the post-war years, the working timetable allowed for a daily (Sundays excepted) goods train from Mellis to Eye and back, and the Mellis signalbox register for July 1962 gives an insight into the level of usage at that time. On seven days during that month, there was no traffic on offer, so the train didn't run at all. It did operate on the remaining 19 weekdays, giving a total of 38 single trips over the branch. Seventeen of these conveyed either one or two wagons, fourteen handled between three and six wagons and on the remaining seven trips the train was formed of just an engine and brake van. By now the traffic was neither regular nor, presumably, profitable. (NRS Archive)

116. The goods service was withdrawn from 13th July 1964, and the tracks were subsequently lifted. Nature is taking hold on 22nd May 1966, and the cattle pens have disappeared under the bushes to the right, although a rusting lamp holder still clings to the corner of the goods shed. A visit in 2015 revealed that industrial development had covered the station site. (S.Moore)

3. Diss

XVI. Having returned to Mellis from Eye it was felt that heading the last 3½ miles to Diss would take us to a suitable place to break the journey to Norwich, as it is one of only two stopping points in the 21st century between Ipswich and Norfolk's county town. This 1904 map shows the station area, which was located almost a mile to the east of the town centre.

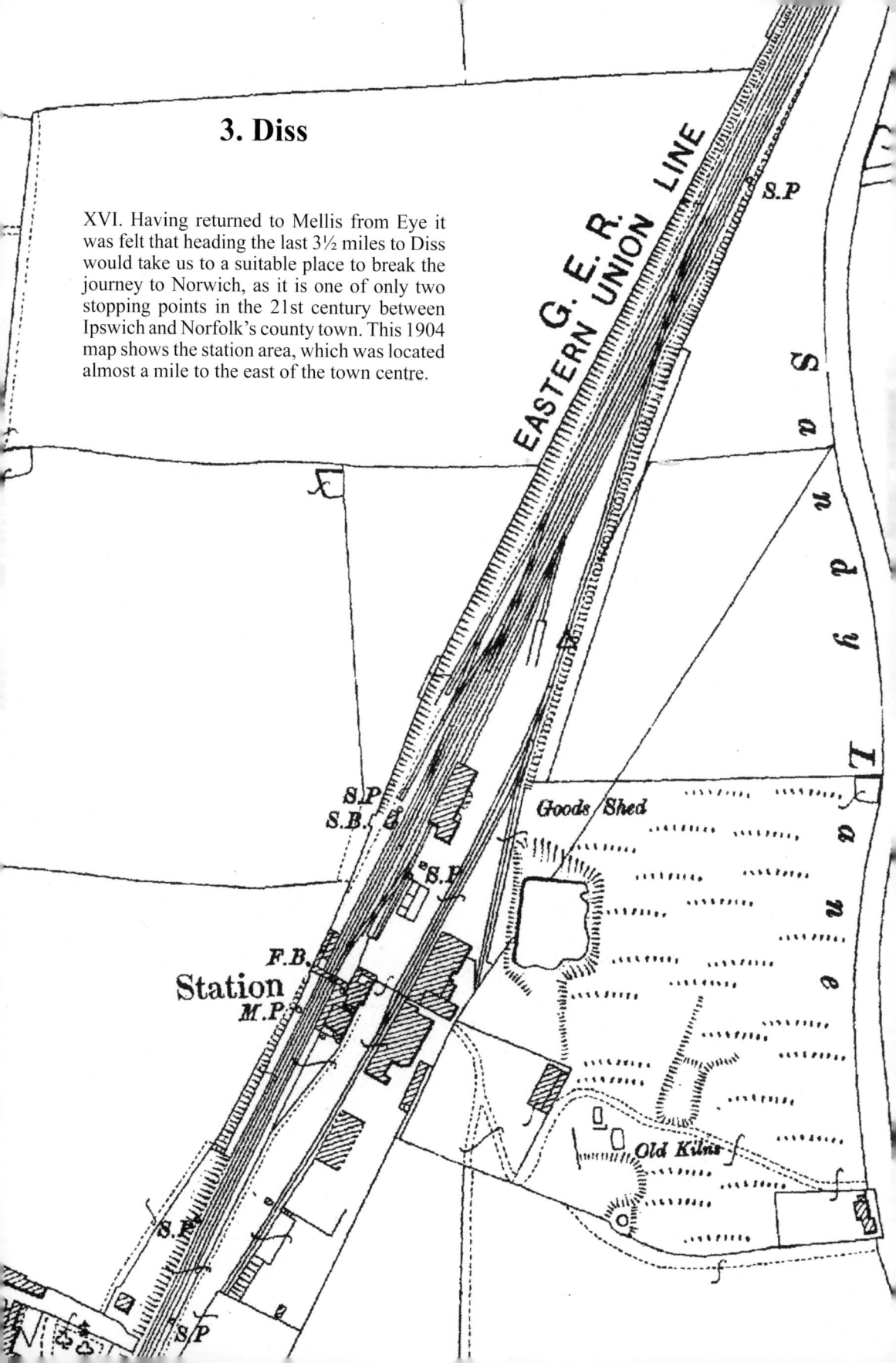

EASTERN UNION LINE

G. E. R.

S.P

Sandy Lane

S.P

S.B.

S.P

Goods Shed

F.B.

Station

M.P.

S.P

Old Kilns

S.P

117. With the three men on the platform seemingly more interested in the cameraman, a GER 4-4-0 heads an up train through the station in the early years of the twentieth century. The description on this postcard, postmarked September 1908, states "Cromer Express (60 miles an hour) passing through Diss" and is a reminder that the Cromer traffic was very important to the Great Eastern Railway in the early 20th century. (Philip Standley collection)

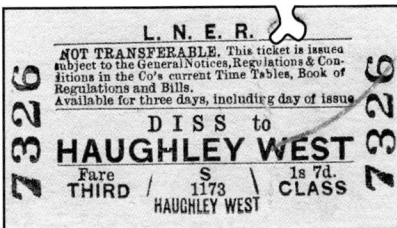

118. During the 1950s, class B1 4-6-0 no. 61109 steams north through the station with a goods train, formed largely of milk tank wagons. The platforms were still gas-lit at this time. (Milepost 92½)

OUT		CL TYPE	FARE PAID
	022	2PS	T 0- 2-0

British Rail *Inter-City*

DISS	
AND	ISSUING OFFICE
IPSWICH	British Rail (E) Diss

VALIDITY OF TICKET TYPES:
CODE O.S. (ORDINARY SGLE) 3 DAYS
CODE O.R. (ORDINARY RTN) 3 MONTHS
OTHER CODES - AS ADVERTISED

ISSUED SUBJECT TO THE REGULATIONS AND CONDITIONS IN THE PUBLICATIONS AND NOTICES OF THE BRITISH RAILWAYS BOARD

NOT TRANSFERABLE. GOOD FOR TRAVEL ONLY WHEN VALIDATED IN THIS SPACE

DATE OF ISSUE	TICKET No.
17 MAY 69	1 176

VALID FOR SINGLE JOURNEY ONLY
RETURN

119. We are looking northwards along the up platform during the late 1950s, and the place still has an unhurried rural atmosphere, with open countryside to the west. There are milk churns on a trolley on the platform, and others on the lorry visible behind the railings. (NRS Archive)

120. No. 90012 runs into the platform with a train from Norwich on 15th April 2015. A comparison with picture 117 will reveal that the main building and canopy have changed little in over a century. (R.J.Adderson)

MP Middleton Press

EVOLVING THE ULTIMATE RAIL ENCYCLOPEDIA

Easebourne Lane, Midhurst, West Sussex.
GU29 9AZ Tel:01730 813169
www.middletonpress.co.uk email:info@middletonpress.co.uk

A-978 0 906520 B- 978 1 873793 C- 978 1 901706 D-978 1 904474
E - 978 1 906008 F - 978 1 908174

All titles listed below were in print at time of publication - please check current availability by looking at our website - *www.middletonpress.co.uk* or by requesting a Brochure which includes our *LATEST* RAILWAY TITLES also our TRAMWAY, TROLLEYBUS, MILITARY and COASTAL series

A
Abergavenny to Merthyr C 91 8
Abertillery & Ebbw Vale Lines D 84 5
Aberystwyth to Carmarthen E 90 1
Allhallows - Branch Line to A 62 8
Alton - Branch Lines to A 11 6
Andover to Southampton A 82 6
Ascot - Branch Lines around A 64 2
Ashburton - Branch Line to B 95 4
Ashford - Steam to Eurostar B 67 1
Ashford to Dover A 48 2
Austrian Narrow Gauge D 04 3
Avonmouth - BL around D 42 5
Aylesbury to Rugby D 91 3

B
Baker Street to Uxbridge D 90 6
Bala to Llandudno E 87 1
Banbury to Birmingham D 27 2
Banbury to Cheltenham E 63 5
Bangor to Holyhead F 01 7
Bangor to Portmadoc E 72 7
Barking to Southend C 80 2
Barmouth to Pwllheli E 53 6
Barry - Branch Lines around D 50 0
Bartlow - Branch Lines to F 27 7
Bath Green Park to Bristol C 36 9
Bath to Evercreech Junction A 60 4
Beamish 40 years on rails E94 9
Bedford to Wellingborough D 31 9
Berwick to Drem F 64 2
Berwick to St. Boswells F 75 8
B'ham to Tamworth & Nuneaton F 63 5
Birkenhead to West Kirby F 61 1
Birmingham to Wolverhampton E253
Bletchley to Cambridge D 94 4
Bletchley to Rugby E 07 9
Bodmin - Branch Lines around B 83 1
Boston to Lincoln F 80 2
Bournemouth to Evercreech Jn A 46 8
Bournemouth to Weymouth A 57 4
Bradshaw's History F18 5
Bradshaw's Rail Times 1850 F 13 0
Bradshaw's Rail Times 1895 F 11 6
Branch Lines series - see town names
Brecon to Neath D 43 2
Brecon to Newport D 16 6
Brecon to Newtown E 06 2
Brighton to Eastbourne A 16 1
Brighton to Worthing A 03 1
Bristol to Taunton D 03 6
Bromley South to Rochester B 23 7
Bromsgrove to Birmingham D 87 6
Bromsgrove to Gloucester D 73 9
Broxbourne to Cambridge F16 1
Brunel - A railtour D 74 6
Bude - Branch Line to B 29 9
Burnham to Evercreech Jn B 68 0

C
Cambridge to Ely D 55 5
Canterbury - BLs around B 58 9
Cardiff to Dowlais (Cae Harris) E 47 5
Cardiff to Pontypridd E 95 6
Cardiff to Swansea E 42 0
Carlisle to Hawick E 85 7
Carmarthen to Fishguard E 66 6
Caterham & Tattenham Corner B251
Central & Southern Spain NG E 91 8
Chard and Yeovil - BLs a C 30 7
Charing Cross to Dartford A 75 8
Charing Cross to Orpington A 96 3
Cheddar - Branch Line to B 90 9
Cheltenham to Andover C 43 7
Cheltenham to Redditch D 81 4
Chester to Birkenhead F 21 5
Chester to Manchester F 51 2
Chester to Rhyl E 93 2
Chester to Warrington F 40 6
Chichester to Portsmouth A 14 7
Clacton and Walton - BLs to F 04 8
Clapham Jn to Beckenham Jn B 36 7
Cleobury Mortimer - BLs a E 18 5
Clevedon & Portishead - BLs to D180
Consett to South Shields E 57 4
Cornwall Narrow Gauge D 56 2
Corris and Vale of Rheidol E 65 9
Craven Arms to Llandeilo E 35 2
Craven Arms to Wellington E 33 8
Crawley to Littlehampton A 34 5
Crewe to Manchester F 57 4
Cromer - Branch Lines around C 26 0
Croydon to East Grinstead B 48 0
Crystal Palace & Catford Loop B 87 1
Cyprus Narrow Gauge E 13 0

D
Darjeeling Revisited F 09 3
Darlington Leamside Newcastle E 28 4
Darlington to Newcastle D 98 2
Dartford to Sittingbourne B 34 3
Denbigh - Branch Lines around F 32 1
Derwent Valley - BL to the D 06 7
Devon Narrow Gauge E 09 3
Didcot to Banbury D 02 9
Didcot to Swindon C 84 0
Didcot to Winchester C 13 0
Dorset & Somerset NG D 76 0
Douglas - Laxey - Ramsey E 75 8
Douglas to Peel C 88 8
Douglas to Port Erin C 55 0
Douglas to Ramsey D 39 5
Dover to Ramsgate A 78 9
Dublin Northwards in 1950s E 31 4
Dunstable - Branch Lines to E 27 7

E
Ealing to Slough C 42 0
Eastbourne to Hastings A 27 7
East Cornwall Mineral Railways D 22 7
East Croydon to Three Bridges A 53 6
Eastern Spain Narrow Gauge E 56 7
East Grinstead - BLs to A 07 9
East London - Branch Lines of C 44 4
East London Line B 80 0
East of Norwich - Branch Lines E 69 7
Effingham Junction - BLs a A 74 1
Ely to Norwich C 90 1
Enfield Town & Palace Gates D 32 6
Epsom to Horsham A 30 7
Eritrean Narrow Gauge E 38 3
Euston to Harrow & Wealdstone C 89 5
Exeter to Barnstaple B 15 2
Exeter to Newton Abbot C 49 9
Exeter to Tavistock B 69 5
Exmouth - Branch Lines to B 00 8

F
Fairford - Branch Line to A 52 9
Falmouth, Helston & St. Ives C 74 1
Fareham to Salisbury A 67 3
Faversham to Dover B 05 3
Felixstowe & Aldeburgh - BL to D 20 3
Fenchurch Street to Barking C 20 8
Festiniog - 50 yrs of enterprise C 83 3
Festiniog 1946-55 E 01 7
Festiniog in the Fifties B 68 8
Festiniog in the Sixties B 91 6
Ffestiniog in Colour 1955-82 F 25 3
Finsbury Park to Alexandra Pal C 02 8
Frome to Bristol B 77 0

G
Galashiels to Edinburgh F 52 9
Gloucester to Bristol D 35 7
Gloucester to Cardiff D 66 1
Gosport - Branch Lines around A 36 9
Greece Narrow Gauge D 72 2

H
Hampshire Narrow Gauge D 36 4
Harrow to Watford D 14 2
Harwich & Hadleigh - BLs to F 02 4
Harz Revisited F 62 8
Hastings to Ashford A 37 6
Hawick to Galashiels F 36 9
Hawkhurst - Branch Line to A 66 6
Hayling - Branch Line to A 12 3
Hay-on-Wye - BL around D 92 0
Haywards Heath to Seaford A 28 4
Hemel Hempstead - BLs to D 88 3
Henley, Windsor & Marlow - BLa C77 2
Hereford to Newport D 54 8
Hertford & Hatfield - BLs a E 58 1
Hertford Loop E 71 0
Hexham to Carlisle D 75 3
Hexham to Hawick F 08 6
Hitchin to Peterborough D 07 4
Holborn Viaduct to Lewisham A 81 9
Horsham - Branch Lines to A 02 4
Huntingdon - Branch Line to A 93 2

I
Ilford to Shenfield C 97 0
Ilfracombe - Branch Line to B 21 3
Industrial Rlys of the South East A 09 3
Ipswich to Diss F 81 9
Ipswich to Saxmundham C 41 3
Isle of Wight Lines - 50 yrs C 12 3
Italy Narrow Gauge F 17 8

K
Kent Narrow Gauge C 45 1
Kettering to Nottingham F 82-6
Kidderminster to Shrewsbury E 10 9
Kingsbridge - Branch Line to C 98 7
Kings Cross to Potters Bar E 62 8
King's Lynn to Hunstanton F 58 1
Kingston & Hounslow Loops A 83 3
Kingswear - Branch Line to C 17 8

L
Lambourn - Branch Line to C 70 3
Launceston & Princetown - BLs C 19 2
Lewisham to Dartford A 92 5
Lincoln to Cleethorpes F 56 7
Lines around Wimbledon B 75 6
Liverpool Street to Chingford D 01 2
Liverpool Street to Ilford C 34 5
Llandeilo to Swansea E 46 8
London Bridge to Addiscombe B 20 6
London Bridge to East Croydon A 58 1
Longmoor - Branch Lines to A 41 3
Looe - Branch Line to C 22 2
Loughborough to Nottingham F 68 0
Lowestoft - BLs around E 40 6
Ludlow to Hereford E 14 7
Lydney - Branch Lines around E 26 0
Lyme Regis - Branch Line to A 45 1
Lynton - Branch Line to B 04 6

M
Machynlleth to Barmouth E 54 3
Maesteg and Tondu Lines E 06 2
Majorca & Corsica Narrow Gauge F 41 3
March - Branch Lines around B 09 1
Market Drayton - BLs around F 67 3
Marylebone to Rickmansworth D 49 4
Melton Constable to Yarmouth Bch E031
Midhurst - Branch Lines of E 78 9
Midhurst - Branch Lines to F 00 0
Minehead - Branch Line to A 80 2
Mitcham Junction Lines B 01 5
Monmouth - Branch Lines to E 20 8
Monmouthshire Eastern Valleys D 71 5
Moretonhampstead - BL to C 27 7
Moreton-in-Marsh to Worcester D 26 5
Mountain Ash to Neath D 80 7

N
Newark to Doncaster F 78 9
Newbury to Westbury C 66 6
Newcastle to Hexham D 69 2
Newport (IOW) - Branch Lines to A 26 0
Newquay - Branch Lines to C 71 0
Newton Abbot to Plymouth C 60 4
Newtown to Aberystwyth E 41 3
North East German NG D 44 9
Northern Alpine Narrow Gauge F 37 6
Northern France Narrow Gauge C 75 8
Northern Spain Narrow Gauge E 83 3
North London Line B 94 7
North of Birmingham F 55 0
North Woolwich - BLs around C 65 9
Nottingham to Boston F 70 3
Nottingham to Lincoln F 43 7

O
Ongar - Branch Line to E 05 5
Orpington to Tonbridge B 03 9
Oswestry - Branch Lines around E 60 4
Oswestry to Whitchurch E 81 9
Oxford to Bletchley D 57 9
Oxford to Moreton-in-Marsh D 15 9

P
Paddington to Ealing C 37 6
Paddington to Princes Risborough C819
Padstow - Branch Line to B 54 1
Pembroke and Cardigan - BLs to F 29 1
Peterborough to Kings Lynn E 32 1
Peterborough to Newark F 72 7
Plymouth - BLs around B 98 5
Plymouth to St. Austell C 63 5
Pontypool to Mountain Ash D 65 4
Pontypridd to Merthyr F 14 7
Pontypridd to Port Talbot E 86 4
Porthmadog 1954-94 - BLa B 31 2
Portmadoc 1923-46 - BLa B 13 8
Portsmouth to Southampton A 31 4
Portugal Narrow Gauge E 67 3
Potters Bar to Cambridge D 70 8
Princes Risborough - BL to D 05 0
Princes Risborough to Banbury C 85 7

R
Railways to Victory C 16 1
Reading to Basingstoke B 27 5
Reading to Didcot C 79 6
Reading to Guildford A 47 5
Redhill to Ashford A 73 4
Return to Blaenau 1970-82 C 64 2
Rhyl to Bangor F 15 4
Rhymney & New Tredegar Lines E 48 2
Rickmansworth to Aylesbury D 61 6
Romania & Bulgaria NG E 23 9
Romneyrail C 32 1
Ross-on-Wye - BLs around E 30 7
Ruabon to Barmouth E 84 0
Rugby to Birmingham E 37 6
Rugby to Loughborough F 12 3
Rugby to Stafford F 07 9
Ryde to Ventnor A 19 2

S
Salisbury to Westbury B 39 8
Sardinia and Sicily Narrow Gauge F 50 5
Saxmundham to Yarmouth C 69 7
Saxony & Baltic Germany Revisited F 71 0
Saxony Narrow Gauge D 47 0
Seaton & Sidmouth - BLs to A 95 6
Selsey - Branch Line to A 04 8
Sheerness - Branch Line to B 16 2
Shenfield to Ipswich E 96 3
Shrewsbury - Branch Line to A 86 4
Shrewsbury to Chester E 70 3
Shrewsbury to Crewe F 48 2
Shrewsbury to Ludlow E 21 5
Shrewsbury to Newtown E 29 1
Sierra Leone Narrow Gauge D 28 9
Sirhowy Valley Line E 12 3
Sittingbourne to Ramsgate A 90 1
Slough to Newbury C 56 7
South African Two-foot gauge E 51 2
Southampton to Bournemouth A 42 0
Southend & Southminster BLs E 76 5
Southern Alpine Narrow Gauge F 22 2
Southern France Narrow Gauge C 47 5
South London Line B 46 6
South Lynn to Norwich City F 03 1
Southwold - Branch Line to A 15 4
Spalding - Branch Lines around E 52 9
Spalding to Grimsby F 65 9 6
Stafford to Chester F 34 5
Stafford to Wellington F 59 8
St Albans to Bedford D 08 1
St. Austell to Penzance C 67 3
St. Boswell to Berwick F 44 4
Steaming Through Isle of Wight
Steaming Through West Hants
Stourbridge to Wolverhampton
St. Pancras to Barking D 68 5
St. Pancras to Folkestone E 88
St. Pancras to St. Albans C 78
Stratford to Cheshunt F 53 6
Stratford-u-Avon to Birmingham
Stratford-u-Avon to Cheltenham
Sudbury - Branch Lines to F 19
Surrey Narrow Gauge C 87 1
Sussex Narrow Gauge C 68 0
Swanley to Ashford B 45 9
Swansea - Branch Lines around
Swansea to Carmarthen E 59 8
Swindon to Bristol C 96 3
Swindon to Gloucester D 46 3
Swindon to Newport D 30 2
Swiss Narrow Gauge C 94 9

T
Talyllyn 60 E 98 7
Tamworth to Derby F 76 5
Taunton to Barnstaple B 60 2
Taunton to Exeter C 82 6
Taunton to Minehead F 39 0
Tavistock to Plymouth B 88 6
Tenterden - Branch Line to A 21
Three Bridges to Brighton A 35
Tilbury Loop C 86 4
Tiverton - BLs around C 62 8
Tivetshall to Beccles D 41 8
Tonbridge to Hastings A 44 4
Torrington - Branch Lines to B 3
Towcester - BLs around E 39 0
Tunbridge Wells BLs A 32 1

U
Upwell - Branch Line to B 64 0

V
Victoria to Bromley South A 98
Victoria to East Croydon A 40 6
Vivarais Revisited E 08 6

W
Walsall Routes F 45 1
Wantage - Branch Line to D 25
Wareham to Swanage 50 yrs D
Waterloo to Windsor A 54 3
Waterloo to Woking A 38 3
Watford to Leighton Buzzard D 4
Wellingborough to Leicester F 7
Welshpool to Llanfair E 49 9
Wenford Bridge to Fowey C 09
Westbury to Bath B 55 8
Westbury to Taunton C 76 5
West Cornwall Mineral Rlys D 4
West Croydon to Epsom B 08 4
West German Narrow Gauge D
West London - BLs of C 50 5
West London Line B 84 8
West Wiltshire - BLs of D 12 8
Weymouth - BLs A 65 9
Willesden Jn to Richmond B 71
Wimbledon to Beckenham C 58
Wimbledon to Epsom B 62 6
Wimborne - BLs around A 97 0
Wisbech - BLs around C 01 7
Witham & Kelvedon - BLs a E 8
Woking to Alton A 59 8
Woking to Portsmouth A 25 3
Woking to Southampton A 55 0
Wolverhampton to Shrewsbury
Wolverhampton to Stafford F 79
Worcester to Birmingham D 97
Worcester to Hereford D 38 8
Worthing to Chichester A 06 2
Wrexham to New Brighton F 47
Wroxham - BLs around F 31 4

Y
Yeovil - 50 yrs change C 38 3
Yeovil to Dorchester A 76 5
Yeovil to Exeter A 91 8
York to Scarborough F 23 9